DATE DUE

DEC 6 – 1995	
DEC 2 0 1995	
JAN 0 4 1996	
MAY – 9 1996	
JUL 2 2 1997	
NOV 3 0 2000	
APR 2 0 2001	
JAN 0 6 2003	
JAN 2 0 2003	
FEB 2 4 2003	

BRODART   Cat. No. 23-221

Living
As
If

Sarah R. Taggart

Living As If

Belief Systems in Mental Health Practice

Jossey-Bass Publishers
San Francisco

Substantial discounts on bulk quantities of Jossey-Bass books are available to corporations, professional associations, and other organizations. For details and discount information, contact the special sales department at Jossey-Bass Inc., Publishers. (415) 433–1740; Fax (415) 433–0499.

For sales outside the United States, contact Maxwell Macmillan International Publishing Group, 866 Third Avenue, New York, New York 10022.

Manufactured in the United States of America. Nearly all Jossey-Bass books, jackets, and periodicals are printed on recycled paper that contains at least 50 percent recycled waste, including 10 percent postconsumer waste. Many of our materials are also printed with vegetable-based ink; during the printing process these inks emit fewer volatile organic compounds (VOCs) than petroleum-based inks. VOCs contribute to the formation of smog.

Library of Congress Cataloging-in-Publication Data

Taggart, Sarah R., date.
    Living as if: belief systems in mental health practice/Sarah R. Taggart.
    p. cm.—(The Jossey-Bass social and behavioral science series)
    Includes bibliographical references and index.
    ISBN 1-55542-652-2
    1. Psychology and religion. 2. Psychiatry and religion.
    3. Mental health—Religious aspects. 4. Belief and doubt.
I. Title. II. Series.
BF51.T34   1994
150' . 1—dc20   93-45033
                                             CIP

FIRST EDITION
HB Printing   10 9 8 7 6 5 4 3 2 1   Code 9449

The Jossey-Bass
Social and Behavioral Science Series

Contents

Part Two
RELIGION AND MENTAL HEALTH

Preface

The premise of this book is that every person has a set of "core beliefs" about the nature of reality and lives *as if* certain absolutes were true. However, as professionals, we in mental health practice have somewhat unquestioningly accepted the reality assumptions of science, and competing core beliefs such as those of religion have made us uncomfortable to the extent that we have usually excluded them from professional literature and traditional practice modalities. I contend that we have thereby excluded a vast and important arena of human experience and a potentially huge clientele in need of our services.

In the history of our profession, words like *religion*, *God*, *mystery*, and *spirituality* have borne such a stigma of professional embarrassment that it is possible to scan the indexes of many mental health texts without finding any of these words listed. Even now we can feel the tension in the room rise when, at a staff meeting or a professional presentation, the subject of religion or spirituality comes up. As with discussions of politics, we know before we begin that we are dealing with a subject about which people have passionate feelings and about which they will inevitably disagree. The reasons for the passion, the nature of these disagreements, and some practical and theoretical suggestions for resolving them constitute my primary subject matter.

We have lived for several hundred years with the assumption that reality can be understood and altered only by the applied sciences. Biology and its stepchild, psychology, have been presented as vehicles for modifying human experience, and we have dismissed religion as belonging to the dream world of superstition and magic—irrelevant if not harmful, of a different order from scientific fact. But I will be arguing throughout this discussion that psychology and religion are two sides of the same coin and that both deal with the same existential realities, with dimensions and consistencies that can be described and even experimented with. The language and goals of psychology and religion may differ, but there are areas of this-world reality on which both conceptually agree.

My hope is to provoke mental health professionals into rethinking their own and their clients' core beliefs in order to provide a rationale for incorporating spiritual and religious concerns into mental health practices. I will be arguing that our core beliefs underlie everything about us and should be considered outside the conventional frameworks of psychological causality—that they are ubiquitous, are sometimes secular and sometimes religious, and have a purpose and structure that can be examined and understood. I ask you to examine the ways in which your own core beliefs intersect with those of your clients, and I suggest that discomfort with beliefs very different from our own has caused us to bracket off an important dimension of human life, "religion" in the broadest sense of the word.

The theoretical basis for this discussion comes from the observation that one of the greatest changes of the late twentieth century is the reopening of questions about the nature of reality. What seemed so certain one hundred years ago—that science could explain our world and ourselves—no longer seems obvious. Although this new uncertainty in some sense leaves us without the secure existential footing we once thought we had, it also opens up the possibility for new models and paradigms in the psychological world just as it does in the physical world. However untidy such new concepts may be, in the realm of human imagination and affect (the realms within which mental health professionals operate) they are frequently the bedrock on which our clients stand, the wellsprings that quench their spiritual longings.

The effort to create a scientific psychology, in combination with a sometimes rigid "separation of church and state" orthodoxy in training institutions and universities, has meant an almost total lack of dialogue between mental health practice and larger philosophical considerations, especially when philosophy spills over into theology. This is a philosophy book to the extent that *philosophy* means examining how and why we think. But philosophy itself has been guilty of attempting to be a "science," and so to the extent that this discussion deals with the ephemeral, the metaphorical, and the universal, it is also a theology book.

Am I transgressing into forbidden realms? My intention is to hold all systems of belief in equal esteem, though I acknowledge that in our personal lives we unavoidably choose particular belief systems within which to live. I do not intend this as an apology for any particular religion or belief system. I merely ask you to consider the possibility that if you are teaching your students to work with the "whole person," you give them the tools to deal both intellectually and practically with the aspect of the whole person that we call "belief." As I will explain in more detail, that does not necessarily mean a religion (though of course it may) but rather refers to those inevitable and unavoidable assumptions we all have to make about the nature of reality.

I come to this project out of the conviction that there is a great longing within the mental health professions—psychiatry, psychology, social work, pastoral counseling, lay counseling, and psychiatric nursing—to include what is often called the *spiritual* in our theoretical and methodological literature, and I hope that this book will begin to provide a framework for a broader definition of mental health practice. As I will attempt to demonstrate, when our ambitions expand to include a much wider population, we are challenged to expand our philosophical base as well. My conception of mental health practice includes as its clientele anyone who is suffering from accidents of fate, social injustice, personality disorder, interpersonal conflict, or developmental stress. I assume that our goal is always the relief of suffering and that our strategies should be as varied as our clientele. It always saddened me when my social work students aspired to "private practice"; though I have great respect for psychotherapy, I consider it a specialty, and I rejoice when mental health practice as a whole is taken out of the office and into the world. But we have always known that when we do this, we must respect and understand life-styles different from our own, and I am advocating here a deeper respect for beliefs different from our own as well.

Since my own belief system, which I will not be able to conceal, may intersect with yours in irritating ways (we are all defensive about our core beliefs), your reaction thus becomes an illustration of what can happen in a specific treatment situation when client and therapist have differing core beliefs. I will ask you to notice when this occurs and to consider its source. I have tried to illustrate how sensitivity to belief systems affects mental health practice by using cases from my professional experience as well as from my own life. I am a fervent advocate of "therapist transparency," and one of my premises is that we give clients permission to share sensitive and frightening material to the extent that we are willing to do so ourselves. And nothing is more sensitive or more frightening to examine than our assumptions about reality—in fact, many readers may object to my use of the word *assumptions*, being convinced that they "know" what is "real." It is from such knowing that the title of this book derives, considering that, as I said, each of us (there are no exceptions) lives *as if* certain premises about reality were true.

In my own life experience I had found it necessary to hide my spiritual longings both personally and professionally until late middle age because, in the era of my own education and psychological acculturation, "maturity" was equated with "good reality testing," and religion wasn't "real." But somewhat to my confusion and embarrassment, I became preoccupied with religious philosophy after a brush with death in my late teens, and my only way of interpreting this obsession was to view it as a dependency on childish illusions—exactly as my parents and, later, my college professors viewed it.

Apparently I had had tuberculosis throughout my childhood, and it was finally diagnosed when I was seventeen years old, during a time when TB was one of the leading causes of death in the world and when there was no treatment except bed rest and various unpleasant forms of surgery. In those days TB patients were hospitalized, not for weeks or months only, but sometimes for decades.

My own severely restrictive hospitalizations lasted two years during the first episode and another year after my second child was born. Overall it was an extended experience that wonderfully focused my mind on ultimate questions. The TB experiences also instilled in me some powerful convictions about professional practice: medical, psychological, religious, even educational. The professionals in my own gallery of saints were without exception vulnerable human beings first, valuing kindness, honesty, and personal openness.

My professional career was in clinical social work and social work education. A personal midlife crisis caused me abruptly to shut the door on both therapy practice and teaching and finally to indulge my fascination with theology by entering a Doctor of Ministry program. But oddly enough, concurrent with my religious studies, I also began an excellent psychoanalytical therapy, and to my surprise I found that the two enterprises were wonderfully complementary. Before this happy experience I had had encounters with colleagues, therapists, and teachers who had managed so thoroughly to discount religious sensibilities of any kind that if I revealed my own, my colleagues were benignly tolerant at best and ridiculing at worst. Rarely, and never formally, were my religious yearnings valued and affirmed. I have become convinced that the discounting I have just described was the result, not of insensitivity or unkindness, but of a particular professional mind-set created by what I am convinced is an obsolete attempt to have a "scientific" understanding of human psychology. My education was saturated with this mind-set, and so, I imagine, was yours. I hope to demonstrate that we can be professionally accountable and still elicit and encourage beliefs other than our own.

Audience

Though this discussion is directed primarily to practitioners in the world of mental health, by whatever name they call themselves, I hope it will intrigue seekers and questioners in the larger community as well. It is my hope that it will be read by anyone who has felt frustrated by the chilly detachment involved in dealing with behavior and emotion without attention to the spiritual—the soul, the ineffable, that mysterious connection to whatever is "More"— particularly pastoral counselors who have begun to question their own unique point of view in an effort to be "scientific." In addition, I hope this discussion will make its way into both mental health and seminary classrooms as a supplement to basic assessment and intervention texts, though it is not intended as a substitute for the fundamentals.

Overview of the Contents

The book is divided into two parts. The first part covers the nature of belief systems in general and suggests ways in which different belief systems can be applied to mental health practice. Chapter One introduces the concept of "belief systems" as differentiated from "religion." Chapters Two and Three examine how and why people have belief systems, and Chapter Four suggests what belief systems consist of. Chapter Five expands the concept to include the notion of living as if certain aspects of reality were true and studies the application of beliefs to questions of alternative realities, ethics, and anthropology. Chapters Six, Seven, and Eight review some specific "as ifs" in the secular, psychological, and religious worlds, and Chapters Nine and Ten take the discussion into the practical realm of mental health practice.

The second part of the book deals specifically with religious beliefs and institutions as they relate to mental health. In Chapter Eleven I argue for the importance of the world religions in the lives of our clients, and in Chapters Twelve and Thirteen I describe the nature and purpose of institutional religions, attempting to differentiate between "religions" and "cults." I note how stereotyping and projecting have clouded our understanding of religions other than our own, and I provide a broad description of the major religions in the United States. I take up the question of the difference between religious experience and mental illness in Chapter Fourteen and in Chapter Fifteen survey some new practice modalities that seem to provide opportunities for the inclusion of spiritual concerns in treatment. The final chapter is a consideration of the opportunities and challenges we face.

Acknowledgments

I owe debts of gratitude to a number of people, not least of whom are those professional adversaries whose skepticism about religion has caused me to organize my own thoughts and convictions—if you are reading this, you know who you are, and I thank you very much. I offer a deep bow to Erv and Miriam Polster, who shook me loose from what Erv once called my "profoundly conservative background"; to John Biersdorf at the Ecumenical Theological Center, who enabled me to put my life onto an entirely new course; to Sheila Mason and Mary Lou Theisen, whose wise guidance and careful listening helped me tap into my "wellspring"; and to my dear friend, the late Lee Morical, who once told me that God gives us the time to do what we need to do.

Ann Arbor, Michigan   SARAH R. TAGGART
February 1994

The Author

Sarah R. Taggart is a retired social work clinician and educator. She received her B.A. (1966) in education and her M.S.W. (1969) in casework from the University of Michigan. She has a certificate in Gestalt therapy (1976) from the Gestalt Therapy Center in San Diego and her D.Min. degree (1990) from the Ecumenical Theological Center in Detroit, having written a dissertation on the interface between religion and psychotherapy. Her professional career was with a family agency in Ypsilanti, Michigan, and on the social work faculty at Eastern Michigan University. She was also a licensed marriage counselor and for many years had a private psychotherapy practice in Ann Arbor. Her interest in the subject matter of this book stems from time spent as consultant to a hospice organization and to the Society of Compassionate Friends (bereaved parents), whose local chapter she helped found, and from extensive personal and professional experience with hospitals and nursing homes.

Living
As
If

Part One

—

BELIEF SYSTEMS AND MENTAL HEALTH

Chapter One

⬤

Recognizing Core Beliefs

Once, when I was working as a therapist in a mental health clinic, I was asked to see a young Muslim woman for brief therapy. "The woman specifically asked to see someone who believed in God," the intake worker told me. She hesitated, obviously a little embarrassed. "I understand you are studying Christian theology. I don't know how you would feel about talking to a Muslim." She said she didn't know if the client's request would present an obstacle to therapy, and she was unclear whether or not my avowedly Christian background would be a problem.

The client, Mrs. A., turned out to be a slightly shy, somewhat overweight woman dressed very modestly in Western-style clothes, speaking adequate, if somewhat limited, English. She came to the clinic alone but explained that she had left her small son with a friend, who had driven her there. She herself did not drive. The presenting problem was an episode of shoplifting that had resulted in her arrest. Her husband did not yet know about her offense, but she was due to go to court the following day and was terrified of his reaction when he found out.

"You are afraid of him?" I inquired as gently as I could.

She looked shocked at the idea. "Oh no," she replied. "But he will be angry. He will be disappointed that I could do such a thing. I am the mother of his child. He will not love me."

After a few moments of exploring the details of the shoplifting episode and her relationship to her husband, I asked her about her religious beliefs. "You wanted to see someone who believes in God," I noted.

"Do you believe in God?" she asked me suspiciously.

"Yes I do," I told her. "It's a very important part of my life. It must be important to you too. Are you afraid of God's reaction to your stealing?"

Her eyes filled with tears. "Do you know about my religion?" she inquired. "Stealing, it is a very great sin."

"And is that what's worrying you the most? That God will not forgive you?"

She was visibly relieved that I seemed to understand. I could see her gather herself together to try to explain her religious beliefs to me. She talked about her background and her understanding of what God expected of her. I asked her about the Muslim concept of "sin" and how Muslims could regain God's favor when they sinned. "After all," I observed, "everyone sins sometimes."

She told me she had prayed and prayed about what had happened. I asked her if she felt a response to her prayers, if that was how it worked in her religion. She said she felt that God wanted her to tell her husband. I suggested that perhaps, since she was genuinely sorry, God would be with her during the next several difficult days. She was dubious, but because she felt reassured by my own belief in God, she was willing to give it a try.

When I saw her again the next week, she reported that her husband had indeed been very upset but mainly had wondered over and over again why she had done it. What was wrong that she would need to steal? Didn't she have everything she needed? It seemed to me a very good question, and when we examined it further, it became clear that Mrs. A. felt trapped and in some sense "starved" in a foreign culture where her days consisted of her child, TV, and one or two friends who lived in another town. Above all, she felt alienated from her religion; her husband, a graduate student, was busy and had not found time for the kinds of religious observances that had been central in their lives. She could see, after we talked this over, that the stealing had been a cry for help.

Afterward, my thoughts kept coming back to Mrs. A. Would she have had such a fruitful reconciliation with her husband—he was extremely sympathetic when he understood the entire picture—had I not explored her religious beliefs with her? How much would she have been willing to tell me had I not shared my own beliefs with her? Would her hunger for her own religion have ever surfaced, and if it had not, would the shoplifting have been repeated? Was the shoplifting an effort to participate in materialism—what she perceived to be the "religion" of her new country? What did the intake worker, who was so skeptical about my reaction to a Muslim client, think was going to happen?

For many years I have been troubled by the discomfort with religious beliefs that I perceive within the professional mental health community. I have found myself struck dumb by comments from colleagues such as "I have no use for a religion that sets itself up as the only one" or "My clients would do better to rely more on themselves and less on 'God'!" Setting aside my sense that my colleagues apparently had their own "religion" just as dogmatic as the ones to which they objected, I could never articulate my conviction that we are all entitled to believe what we believe and that somewhere there must be a common meeting ground that would allow us to talk together with respect and understanding. I felt the need to develop an approach to the religious beliefs of clients inclusive enough to encompass a variety of ideas about God and reality.

However, whenever I brought this need up with colleagues, I discovered that attempts at discussing the interface between religion and psychology led nowhere because there is disagreement on what is real, what human beings are all about, and especially on whether or not God exists. So bringing religion into a discussion about professional mental health practice presents a daunting challenge. Setting aside the classic Freudian objections to religion, even less traditional practitioners raise philosophical as well as psychological questions. The core questions—What is real? What is true? What is good?—keep reasserting themselves, especially the question of what is real. Are dreams real? Is imagination real? Are prayers real? Are our dreams the products of our bodies, or are our bodies the products of our dreams? The questions begin to ask themselves in a sort of through-the-looking-glass way.

And of course there are further questions. How do we tell when religion is "harmful"? How can we sort out "good" and "bad" in various religious beliefs? How can we reconcile our own beliefs with beliefs that are different? Why do we each think ours are "right"? Why is religion not simply a psychological response to the scary unknowns in life? All of these concerns are germane.

I began to ask acquaintances for suggestions of persons and projects to investigate. These soon separated themselves into two areas. The first were pastors who were doing therapy, frequently in settings with other sectarian counselors but sometimes in secular mental health clinics and sometimes in association with churches. After talking with many of these people, I concluded that psychotherapy was being practiced by more and more clergy but that it had very little religious or spiritual content. When I interviewed therapists who were suggested to me as combining religion and psychology, I discovered that here, too, spiritual needs tended to disappear under the pressure of psychological distress. Thinking that perhaps ministers were dealing with spiritual needs in their everyday pastoring encounters, I began to inquire about how these sessions were conducted and again learned that psychological needs tended to be preeminent.

When I began to interview persons involved in teaching clinical pastoral education courses in seminaries and to read the texts for such courses, I discovered that excellent introductions to clinical knowledge were available but that they hardly differed from the texts and course content we used when I was teaching assessment and intervention skills to social work students. When I talked with many pastor friends, I realized that they were already knowledgeable about the mental health of their parishioners. It soon became evident to me that there was an extensive literature on the subject of the interface between religion and psychology. Carl Jung, Anton Boisen, John Sanford, Morton Kelsey, Gerald May, Tilden Edwards, Kenneth Leech, Scott Peck, and many others had gotten there long before I had even considered the questions. The whole field of clinical pastoral education was attempting to address them.

I also began to meet therapists who were centrally interested in the spiritual dimensions of therapy, and I increasingly heard about associations of psychotherapists who define themselves as

"Christian" or who operate in specifically Christian or Jewish settings. I found some very good literature on the meaning of religion in personality development—especially, but not exclusively, Jungian—and I became aware that there is more and more willingness on the part of therapists to be sensitive to religious beliefs.

But I continued to be surprised by the somewhat closed worlds in which everyone seemed to operate. The concept "belief systems" was outside the framework of everyone's concern, no matter who the helping professional was, and even ministers seemed leery of stirring their personal belief convictions into their counseling practices. In spite of what appeared to be widespread interest, my final impression was that there was very little genuine combining of the spiritual and the psychological. So my original plan to explore the methods and theories of persons who successfully combined spiritual practices with psychological intervention ran aground on the shoals of the apparent lack of practitioners who held both concerns in more or less equal balance.

In some ways it seemed to me that the problem was the medical model, the one-on-one encounters in which there is a "sick person" and a "healer." The seemingly obvious sentence with which M. Scott Peck begins The Road Less Traveled (1978)—"Life is difficult"—tended to be overlooked when vague ideals of "mental health" prevailed. And yet the astonishing success of Peck's book suggests that most people do in fact understand that life is inevitably difficult and that they welcome a spiritual approach to their life struggles, an approach in which transcendent values are acknowledged and self-discipline and love are respected. Still, it remains true that when crises occur and people are feeling miserable and frightened, they frequently see themselves as "sick" and turn to "helping professionals" to make them well. This is sometimes appropriate.

It finally occurred to me that even defining what we were talking about was a big part of the problem. Within any religion can be found a wide variety of beliefs. Most of the time in this discussion I will be talking about belief systems, the set of assumptions about reality that govern a person's life, rather than about organized religion per se. Whereas our basic beliefs depend on our life experience, our talents and limitations, and the traumas and challenges life dumps on us, our religions are by-products of circumstances—who our parents are, where we were born, what the religions of our larger cultures are—and may or may not reveal what we really believe. For example, Mrs. A.'s origins in a Middle Eastern country virtually guaranteed that she would be Muslim. But her deep belief in God's presence in her life was not necessarily predicted by her formal religious affiliation, and her prayer life had spiritual implications that proved to be important in the solution of her problems.

What each of us assumes about the future in the middle of the night when we are startled into frightened wakefulness by a racing heart is determined illogically and unpredictably by a combination of irrational factors and is largely the product of the unconscious mind. It may or may not have anything to do with our formal religious practices. The form that our urgent need to believe takes in times of emergency varies widely according to the imprint of past religious and spiritual experiences and is, in important ways, unique to us as individuals.

I said in the preface that it is my primary thesis that everyone in the world makes assumptions (has beliefs) about reality. Sometimes those assumptions are cast in religious terms, and sometimes they are not. They are not articulated because most of the time they are unconscious. But they constitute a powerful hidden agenda that influences how we live as well as how we relate to colleagues and clients. Our belief systems undergird everything else about us and provide the color, meaning, and flavor of our lives *whether we are aware of it or not.* Until we understand what someone *believes,* we cannot understand what that person thinks, feels, and does. Furthermore, to the extent that we can clarify and enrich someone's belief system as well as our own, we can live the rest of our lives more fully, *no matter what the belief system is.* Even when it is a destructive system, it can be modified or countered only after it has been understood and in some sense affirmed.

You may be wondering what difference discussion of core beliefs makes to you as a professional. For pastoral counselors, it makes a difference if the insights of psychology are to be of use in a way that does not co-opt religious faith. For mental health professionals, it makes a difference if clients' spiritual quests are to be recognized as crucial to their emotional well-being and affirmed in a way that does not discount them. We need some way of conceiving existence that allows us to listen to viewpoints other than our own with curiosity and respect. This does not require that we agree with them.

As long as personal experience is dichotomized, as it is now, into the psychological (the life of the personality) and the spiritual (invisible life beyond the personality), a common viewpoint is needed to enable practitioners in both worlds to talk to each other. The common viewpoint offered here is appreciation for diversity, mystery, and possibility, a humility that blurs our professional certainties and offers a rationale for the acceptance of the unknown. We do not have to abandon our own beliefs just because we understand the beliefs of someone else. But neither should we insist that others abandon theirs.

Chapter Two

Beliefs as Systems

I realize that for many mental health practitioners, there is something irritatingly vague about talk of belief systems, as if in accepting beliefs of widely varying tenets, they are being asked to lose their rational, analytical minds in a cloud bank. The nice clarity of scientific precepts and experimental models seems to fog over when ideas of God appear, to the extent that many professionals prefer not to think about religious beliefs at all. But some commonly accepted ideas can help us analyze the purposes, structures, and contents of belief systems, and I would like to offer them as organizational aids in assessing our own beliefs and those of clients. It is my hope that by understanding why we need beliefs, how they are structured, and what ideas they contain, we can be more ready to risk crossing over from our own beliefs into the unknowns of someone else's.

Webster's New International Dictionary (1986, p. 2322) defines *system* as "a complex unity formed of many often diverse parts subject to a common plan or serving a common purpose." Beliefs are systems in the sense that their contents (what a person believes) have a certain coherence that depends on basic convictions about the nature of reality, the existence of God, the meaning of life, and the nature of consciousness. As systems, they also have dimensions in common with all other systems: energy sources, distribution of power, input and output, boundaries, and purpose. The last two of these dimensions seem particularly relevant to this discussion.

In addition, to the extent that belief systems, as opposed to systems in general, also deal with the metaphysical and the unknowable, they have qualities that are unique. By definition, they make judgments about what is real and what is good. The ways in which they do this are, I contend, specific to religious beliefs and must be considered by themselves. In the next several chapters, we will examine the purpose of belief systems (*why* people believe), their structure (*how* people believe), and their content (*what* people believe) to see how certain clusters of beliefs belong logically together.

Purposes of Belief Systems

Professor Jeffrey Donner once began a class at St. John's Seminary with the observation that no one knows what reality is. "No one!" he reiterated, pointing a stern finger at us all, lest we fail to grasp the importance of what he was saying. "We arrive in this world with only the certainty that we exist. That's all." He went on to suggest that whether we imagine the rest of the world like a great cosmic dream or whether we are seeds planted in time to grow and develop as best we can without hint or reassurance about our ultimate destinies, we can only guess. Even people who profess mystical experiences of God cannot prove that they are not hallucinating. Whatever we choose to believe about reality, whether it is what our parents taught us, what our culture accepts, or what our intuition suggests to us, our choice is ultimately only an opinion. "So," he added, "what I offer here is my opinion, just as what you choose to believe is your opinion."

Most of us experience a hunger for ultimate meaning in life. We are not content to suspend judgment simply because we cannot prove what we believe. Anyway, it has been observed that people who claim that they have suspended judgment have in practice arbitrarily chosen a reality without meaning, which is a kind of meaning in itself. "Not to choose is to choose," as the popular saying puts it.

Because we have tried to remove subjectivity from respectable science, we have somehow deluded ourselves that it is also important to remove ourselves from the consideration of ultimate questions. Yet, we might ask, are we not central to those questions? Are we betraying Galileo and returning ourselves to the center of the

universe by suggesting that human reason is an important component of reality? For, as many contemporary thinkers have observed,
we know that the universe is not a cosmic clock, a huge sphere
filled with interlocking mechanical parts, however tempting it is
to imagine it that way. Instead it seems to be, above all, a mysterious energy field with laws and relationships far stranger than any
we have previously understood.

In the same way, we have tended to approach our encounters
with one another as if they could be reduced to scientific formulas.
But perhaps it would be useful to return our human exchanges to
where they started, in myth and passion and suffering, where personal experience and religious expression intersect and our everyday lives become our gifts to one another. Because mental health
and philosophy are, in my judgment, inextricably linked, the questions What is a human being? and, even more crucially, What is
reality? are central to both disciplines. Both disciplines question
what happens when we explore the unconscious mind. Do we discover only our deepest self, or is there something more? If there is a
personal God, how does this God communicate with us? If we have
what we think are revelatory experiences, how do we distinguish
them from psychoses?

I will demonstrate how both religious and psychological belief
systems mediate our experiences of reality. I will also point out that
even though personal beliefs are peculiar to each of us individually,
they also depend on certain common dimensions that can be
understood, assessed, and modified. We will briefly examine the
nature of the human awareness that allows us to have beliefs in the
first place and describe how all human beings attempt to cope with
the scary unknowns of life—what have been referred to as *angst* (a
feeling of purposelessness and dread of the unknown) and the
apparent chaos of human experience.

Reducing Angst

Reflect on your own sense of the transitoriness of life. Can you
recall when you first became aware of death? Of fear in an emotionally difficult situation? Of defenselessness when an accident or

sickness threatened your well-being? What messages in your mind enabled you to cope with helplessness and terror? Place those messages in a context. For instance, to distract oneself, one can say, as Scarlett O'Hara did, "I'll think about that in the morning"; that is a good illustration of a sort of nihilistic atheism, as *Gone with the Wind* gives Scarlett no larger belief system than intense loyalty to her home and no source of comfort other than her own quite considerable courage. Or one can think, "I'm going to be all right because God loves me," out of a sense of the divine as protective and beneficent. Whatever the message and the context, we all have evolved individual beliefs, consciously or not, out of the necessity of living in a world without obvious purpose or safety.

The philosopher Rollo May (1983, p. 111) refers to angst as "ontological anxiety," defined as "the experience of the imminent threat of nonbeing." To put it bluntly, our awareness creates the fear of death. May agrees with Ernest Becker (1973) that the fear of death underlies all other fears and is, as Becker says, so scary that intellectuals have tended to rationalize it away. Becker talks about the various methods we have devised to defend ourselves from the fear of nonexistence. He notes that professionals frequently avoid their own fear of death by not attending to the fear presented to them by their clients. But however much we may deny our anxiety, at some level our human self-awareness creates realization of our emergence out of nothing and evident return to nothing.

May explains the nature of existential anxiety in this way:

> In his classical contributions to the understanding of anxiety, Kurt Goldstein has emphasized that anxiety is not something we "have" but something we "are." His vivid descriptions of anxiety at the onset of psychosis, when the patient is literally experiencing the threat of dissolution of the self, make his point abundantly clear. But, as he himself insists, this threat of dissolution of the self is not merely something confined to psychotics but describes the neurotic and normal nature of anxiety as well. Anxiety is the subjective state of the individual's becoming aware that his existence can become destroyed, that he can lose himself and his world, that he can become "nothing" [1983, pp. 109–110].

Our self-awareness causes us to experience angst. It is the sine qua non of human existence; we cannot avoid thinking about the things that happen to us. Without our imagination and our ability to think abstractly, we humans would not be concerned with questions of ultimate destiny and meaning. So we need to examine the nature of human awareness, for it is the amazing ability of our minds to interpret our existence that creates belief systems.

Mediating Chaos

Fortunately, our self-awareness creates not only angst but also the possibility of organizing the barrage of stimuli, ideas, emotions, and memories that constitute individual human life into systems of coherent meaning. In the absence of a system of meaning, this barrage would result in unbearable chaos (as indeed it is experienced by autistic children and by people with certain other psychotic conditions). Therefore, another task of human awareness is the formulation of sets of assumptions with which to mediate this chaos—belief systems into which experiences can be pigeonholed, organized, and in some sense preserved, thus giving us larger categories of relevance to help us interpret and prioritize our experiences.

Human awareness is able to mediate chaos and create meaning because it has another characteristic of particular importance when we consider belief systems: it is primarily analogical and metaphorical. We learn by analogy, building one experience on top of another, thus creating more and more complex structures of thought, and we organize the chaos of existence by constructing metaphors and mental images such as fables, myths, legends, and allegories. We also create complex "selves"—subpersonalities, roles, individualities—out of our ability to extend our own past experience into our understanding of someone else and, conversely, to make the world of the other part of our own. It is that uniquely human ability, imagination, that enables us to create "pictures in our heads" and to project future possibilities from past events (in science at least as much as in psychology and religion). As a consequence, we are endowed by our imaginations with those rich and helpful complexes of assumptions, the belief systems that organize the angst and chaos of our lives.

The Roles of Religion and Psychology

Collective belief systems such as those of religion and psychology also regulate reality through their presuppositions, customs, and dogmas (though I suppose psychologists would prefer not to use the word *dogma* to refer to their precepts). Religious systems reduce angst and mediate chaos through their systems of metaphor and myth—their representations of reality—but also with their rituals, customs, expectations, and mores, which provide reassuring patterns of behavior as well as assurances about the unknown future. As far back as we have evidence of human presence, we have evidence that humans have dealt with existential fear through religious ideas and observances—transcendental frameworks for the reduction of angst.

Psychological systems frequently resemble religions in the sense that their belief systems also serve the purpose of organizing chaos and reducing angst. For example, we are all aware of the many therapists who are as rigidly doctrinaire in their convictions as the most convinced religious believer, and though the best therapists try not to impose their own theories of reality on their patients, it is virtually impossible to be existentially invisible. Mental health models, the ideas on which therapies are based, are intellectual theories intended to tame the surging chaos with which the human personality always seems to be threatened. Indeed, the word *model* seems especially efficacious, suggesting as it does a wealth of raw material that can be shaped and reshaped in an infinite variety of ways.

Concepts of God

Throughout human history, concepts of God (or gods) have been central to the conquest of existential fear. Usually these have been associated with organized religions, but frequently in modern times ideas of God seem to be private and personal, so I would like to consider them separately from collective belief systems.

Discussions of God are particularly difficult for professionals of all kinds to deal with because in the past two centuries, philosophy and science have dismissed concepts of deity as illusionary and contradictory to rational thought. But for the sake of clarity I would like to spend a little time examining how the nature of human awareness affects our general concept of God, realizing that this is a particularly controversial subject but convinced that we can never understand belief systems in general if we dismiss the central precept of so many of them. This will be an argument for a more generous understanding of theological ideas that have historically been discounted and even ridiculed in the mental health world.

To put it in terms we will discuss more fully later, we have no way of knowing how much any concept of God or gods is inner, subjective construct and how much is outer, observable reality. In other words, we do not know to what extent we create God as an idea and to what extent God actually exists. But we do know that in a world of ourselves as "creatures" in the theological sense of the word, our understanding and experience of the Wholly Other, as God has sometimes been called, is limited and conditioned both by our self-awareness and our "creatureliness" (our finiteness, the limits of our sense experiences, and the shortness of our lives). We are thereby condemned by our own limitations to imagine the unfamiliar in terms of the familiar—to cast God in human form.

This is a commentary, not on the existence of God, but rather on the condition of the human imagination. Because this sort of anthropomorphism is frequently cited in intellectual circles as a way to discount ideas of God, it seems critically important to consider the concept in another context. Limited by the images we are able to conceive, we have no way to perceive a God who is unlike ourselves or outside of our experiences. (Even when a religion asserts that the divine "expects" or "requires" some behavior, as was the case with my Muslim client in Chapter One, there is an anthropomorphic aspect to the assertion.) When clients present us with what seems to be a childlike or particularly concrete image of God, they are reflecting their own inner awareness and should not be discounted for this; they are using the mirror of their own experience. An intellectual's concept of God may look entirely different and even seem to escape anthropomorphism altogether, but it is not necessarily more accurate. In fact, when we state that God is entirely "other" than ourselves, for all practical purposes this is a statement without meaning because we are presenting an imageless image.

Our assumptions about God have a profound effect on the way we interact with our clients. If clients assume that life exists in a strictly material universe and mental experiences are merely electrical impulses without any hint of supernatural input, then a perception of themselves as objects alone in the universe, and the importance of physical survival above all, will frame their interactions with the external world. By contrast, those who have ongoing experiences of the transcendental and whose interaction with the world presumes divine intervention will make different assumptions about life, assumptions that will influence their lives in basic ways. This may seem obvious, but I remind you that the reduction of angst and the organization of chaos will be very different depending on presuppositions about the existence of God.

Several examples will suggest how concepts of God motivate our behavior in life-threatening situations and how mental health interventions are thereby altered to accommodate the client's beliefs.

John and Genevieve were a long-married couple whose sternly atheistic beliefs eventually influenced a course of therapy for their adult children. Both John and Genevieve had been handsome, intellectually gifted, and successful for most of their lives, confident of their ability to control the contingencies of fate. They had a belief system based on a sort of Darwinian assumption that the strongest and smartest should prevail. *Virtue* (though that would not have been an acceptable term to them) probably meant taking care of oneself, and *sin* (an even more unacceptable term) would have been equated with weakness and laziness. In general, people got what they deserved, and virtue also demanded that one's weakness not be foisted on anyone else. Genevieve once said to me, "If I ever became helpless, I hope someone would take me out in the backyard and shoot me."

So when, in late middle age, they were both diagnosed with potentially disabling and incurable illnesses—Genevieve with Alzheimer's disease and John with pancreatic cancer—they agreed to commit mutual suicide. The survival task for their adult children, all of whom required mental health interventions to help them deal with the trauma of their parents' death, was to learn gracefully to accept their parents' belief system and to view their suicides as both courageous and gallant within the existential view of reality that they both had held.

At the other extreme was Harry, from an identical background as John and Genevieve but with a diametrically opposite set of existential assumptions. When Harry learned he had a fatal illness, he never wavered in his determination to fight the illness, to remain optimistic, and to lean on his religious faith. He assumed that his illness had some sort of meaning in his life, that God would enable him to bear whatever he was required to bear, and that in the end he would find his way to heaven. Until Harry's last moments of consciousness he remained a fighter, hopeful that somehow a treatment would work or that a cure would be found but confident that whatever happened, he would "triumph." From a conventional mental health perspective, there was a large element of denial in Harry's response to his illness, but surely no professional in any discipline would have wished to interpret that denial or undermine it in any way, and it is a premise of this discussion that in Harry's belief system, denial was a logical and consistent response; indeed, *denial* is an unfortunate term, for it discounts Harry's affirmative belief in God.

Summary

Belief systems are constructs of the human imagination that enable us to cope with the terrors and opportunities of self-awareness.

Belief systems are ubiquitous, unavoidable, and as varied as the various individual minds producing them. Above all, they enable us subconsciously to cope with our dread of nonbeing. The creative myths and metaphors comprising our belief systems are not merely decorative, interesting elaborations that scientifically evolved humanity can live without. They are, rather, the basis for our existence; they are symbol systems that enable us to derive meaning from a chaos of stimuli and instincts and to decode the mystery of our existence. Our separate core beliefs, whether secular or religious, anchor us in the dizzying vastness of the great unknown we call *reality*.

Chapter Three

Structures of Belief Systems

In Chapter Two we discussed the underlying, existential purposes of belief systems, their contribution to the management of angst and chaos in human life. Now I want to consider the structures of belief systems to see how structural elements help us regulate our experience—order it, arrange it, and define it.

Because belief systems depend on the human imagination and reflect individual experiences of reality, they cannot be analyzed in strictly cybernetic terms. I assert that secular, psychological, and religious belief systems all depend on certain commonalities that are of particular importance to them as separate categories of systems. Three structural elements (diversity, synergy, and boundary maintenance) seem to me to be distinguishing characteristics of *all* belief systems, and two are uniquely important to *religious* belief systems (the subject-object split and unity versus duality). It is my hope that by looking at the ways in which beliefs are constructed, we can be more tolerant of the framework, more ready to risk crossing over from the secure structure of our own beliefs into the unknown dwelling of someone else's. I propose to explore these dimensions to provide an analytical basis for counseling practices.

I have said before that belief systems define reality, so before examining them in detail, let me briefly outline three aspects of reality addressed by belief systems in general.

1. Reality is diverse. We will speculate on the importance of diversity; the evolution of the apparently unfinished universe of space, time, matter, and energy (and even consciousness, considered as an additional dimension of reality) is dependent on diversity of all kinds.

2. Reality consists of ever more complex systems. We will consider the nature of complexity, how synergy affects both
   energy and meaning.

3. Reality's differentiations depend on boundaries to prevent
   them from losing their identities. We will consider how
   boundaries affect the sense of self and why an understanding
   of boundary protection undergirds ethics.

Diversity

Essential questions that surface immediately in any discussion of
belief systems are why human beings seem to believe in so many
crazily different things and why it should not be a principle of good
psychology to find a single healthy belief system to which we can
all subscribe. Indeed, I wonder if the mental health profession has
not unconsciously assumed it had just such a system tucked away
in its codes of ethics and its theoretical assumptions. At any rate,
I allege that as a profession, we have not been notably open to the
variety of belief systems with which we are confronted, and since
I am advocating for tolerance, sympathy, and understanding of all
kinds of differing beliefs, I want to make a case here for the importance of system diversity, not only in political systems (where we
do, after all, pay lip service to "pluralities") but also in our assumptions about reality and even, as we will discuss in a moment, in the
very structure of the universe. The variety we observe everywhere
seems to be one of the defining characteristics of human systems:
in addition to our disagreements about religion and psychology, we
seem not to be able to agree on the basics of family life, aesthetics,
politics, or much else. I would like to consider whether this intellectual and emotional diversity is a good thing from a mental
health perspective, and if so, why.

I can perhaps illustrate the problems associated with a unified
(nondiversified) approach by considering what has happened
within our own profession. Not too many years ago, we in the mental health world spoke of "normal" adjustment and behavior, as

though there were one particular absolute against which deviations could be measured. Fortunately, we have largely abandoned the idea of normative psychological standards, but the notion lingers on in the unspoken norms of what in my teaching days we called "mental health values" (the judgments within the psychological community about what is "good"). These consisted of such ideas as the value of individual choice, the value of human dignity, and the value of confidentiality. A "professional" was assumed to subscribe to these values even to the extent that, for instance, confidentiality became a screen for noncooperation of the most egregious kind between workers and "individual choice" came to mean that psychotics sometimes endangered their intimates with only minimum interference from a tolerant mental health profession. So, I would argue, in many ways, even what was hoped to be a unified value system for the overall profession has been seen to suffer from dangerous flaws causing us to qualify and question it.

So what are we to think? Are we just to resign ourselves to what seem to be an absurdly large number of irrational beliefs about the real and the good? My answer is yes. It is a fundamental thesis of this discussion that in beliefs as elsewhere, diversity is not merely to be tolerated but to be valued. As I will explain later, a grand unifying principle seems to be no more likely in psychology than it does in physics, however disappointing that may be to contemplate, and there may be excellent reasons why diversity is the theme of evolution, in human society as in the universe.

Our understanding of reality, that basic purpose of belief systems, can be thought of like the examination of the elephant in the classic story about the committee of blind men who were commissioned to discover what kind of beast had invaded the Valley of the Blind. By putting their hands on different parts of the elephant, they came up with wildly differing descriptions. "The beast is broad and flat and furry," says the man at the animal's side. "No," argues another, who is studying the tail, "it is skinny and slippery." "It is round and has a hole in it," insists the fellow near the trunk. The point of the story is, of course, that they are describing different aspects of the same thing. And that, I insist, is what we do with our beliefs. We describe different aspects of a reality too enormous to encompass in one description. And as with the committee of the blind, if we can learn to listen to one another, we may get a better picture of the whole elephant called reality.

The physicist Freeman Dyson (1988) argues that not only is it useful to have a variety of interpretive lenses through which to view reality, but also it is essential that reality itself be optimally and increasingly diverse. (So when we experience ourselves splintering into new theories and methodologies, perhaps we should applaud, not moan.) Using the largest possible lens, Dyson observes the complexity of the universe and argues that the greater the diversity, the richer the meaning. He believes that the grand multiplicity of creation is central to its apparent purpose. He writes, "There is no such thing as a simple material universe. The old vision which Einstein maintained until the end of his life, of an objective world of space and time and matter independent of human thought and observation, is no longer ours. Einstein hoped to find a universe possessing what he called 'objective reality,' a universe of mountaintops which he could comprehend by means of a finite set of equations. Nature, it turns out, lives not on the mountaintops but in the valleys" (p. 298).

Dyson reminds us that it is the differences between our cells that enable our bodies miraculously to function and the differences between our planetary organisms that enable our ecology miraculously to work. Perhaps, even, it is the differences between us as self-aware creatures that enable us humans to evolve as a species, for if we were all the same and everything worked perfectly, nothing would ever change. Furthermore, Dyson points out, the fact that the universe is full of messy mistakes enables differentiation to occur; evolution would be impossible if there were no failures of organic organisms to adapt to their environments.

We observe this odd paradox even in our mental health systems. When psychoanalysis failed to establish a monolithic therapy system, the way opened for a multiplicity of approaches. I am arguing here that even in our treatment systems, increasing diversity is a positive development, enabling us to address widely varying problems within a variety of psychological belief systems. We can also see the principle of the value of failure in our individual lives. (I acknowledge that this is not a popular idea.) During crisis times, when personal equilibrium is disturbed and our coping strategies fail us, we are forced, whether we like it or not, onto new plateaus of adjustment and understanding, new adaptational expressions of our individuality. Failures are often the reason clients come to us—when a marriage is in trouble, someone has died, or mental illness has undermined normal adjustment. As therapists, we often notice clients becoming more individual, more stubbornly unique, and above all (we hope) more adaptable when forced to bend to unforeseen circumstances. Indeed, speaking in generalities, gerontologists tell us that if we live long enough, we will each become more and more different from everyone else because each of us continuously reinforces our own unique way of adapting to the world. So life itself seems to conspire to increase the diversity within human society.

As a therapist, I notice the virtues of diversity when I think of the sterile futility of working with a client who is a cookie-cutter duplicate of everyone else in his or her environment. I suppose that every therapist has had at least one of these perpetual adolescents who wanted to "be in therapy" because it was what their friends were doing and who thought that a therapist would somehow solve all their problems. Without the knock on the head of a seriously disturbing life crisis, these clients can mumble on through months of psychological masturbation without any perceivable progress or change. Conversely, it is often brave individuals who have survived horrors of tragedy, disappointment, and abuse who can enliven a therapist's day with depths of wisdom and humor that widen one's eyes in amazement.

And diversity not only describes us as individuals; it also applies to the collective makeup of regions, cultures, countries, and groups of all sizes and purposes and presents challenges to our collective mental health that we have not even begun to meet. For a long time, we as a society thought that the "melting pot" was the solution to the conflicts caused by diversity. But there seems to be no acceptable standard of what an ideal, uniform society would look like. The communists thought they had one, and the result was to reduce everyone to the lowest common denominator. The problem persists. Ecumenism, universal public education, modern transportation, and even television have failed to meld us into universal men and women. We remain obstinately ourselves, conservative in the truest sense. The irritations and beauties of our self-protection remain as dangerous as ever, but there seems to be no reason to believe that will ever change. Our belief systems have become, if anything, more disparate than ever, and as we are thrown together in the shrinking world, we are forced to confront our differences, whether we wish to or not.

I contend that one of the major challenges for the mental health community in the next decades will be to broaden our own approaches to practice enough to treat an increasingly eclectic clientele in an increasingly ideological world. In a subsequent chapter I will suggest ways in which a variety of psychological belief systems offers just such theoretical diversity.

Synergy

A particularly puzzling aspect of belief systems is the ferocity with which people cling to them. Rarely can anyone be reasoned out of a firmly held belief. One explanation for this tenacity lies in an aspect of systems of all kinds that the inventor-philosopher Buckminster Fuller (1981) once labeled *synergy*. Fuller noted that a system cannot be defined by reduction to its component parts. A scientist cannot understand you by studying your organs in an X ray or your blood in a test tube. Your personality in some sense defies reduction to the collection of your parts; it has a particular characteristic of its own not conveyed by photographs or blood tests. Fuller used the word *synergy* to describe the purpose and energy accrued by complexities of all kinds. Synergy is the glue that holds complex systems together, and its strength and effectiveness must be taken into account whenever we are considering beliefs of whatever origin. It means, in an oversimplified definition, that the whole is greater than the sum of its parts. If you change a component part, you change the whole system because the *collection* of energy and purpose that we call synergy is thereby changed. But the term also implies that *accrual* is important. For example, the collective energy, wisdom, and motivation of a complex system such as a family can accomplish more difficult tasks than could all the members working separately. The interaction between them creates something completely new, something more distinctive than merely the accumulation of their collective energies.

The same dynamic of synergy occurs with belief systems of all kinds. The moment two people with similar beliefs find each other, what is called a self-reinforcing feedback loop begins. The energy of one person's belief system is reinforced and in some sense enhanced by the energy of the second. When still more "true believers" are added to the system, an institution begins to evolve. The early history of psychoanalysis provides a fascinating illustration of this phenomenon in the world of psychology, and the many cults and denominations deriving from spiritual belief systems are familiar illustrations of the phenomenon in the religious world. We can begin to see why people are so fiercely loyal to whatever institution supports their beliefs, whether the beliefs are religious or secular. The synergy of the collective system has so much more strength and energy than any one of its members—think of the impact of the street gang on the lives of otherwise powerless young men.

Nothing illustrates the strength of synergy better than the antiabortion movement in the United States. It results from a pure belief system (I see very little self-interest or other motivation behind it) and crosses denominational lines; Catholics and fundamentalist Protestants are not usually allies in this way, so it must be beliefs rather than institutional norms that drive the right-to-life organizations. This collective belief system creates a force of impressive effectiveness.

In terms of everyday practice, on the positive side, we could note that whenever isolated, marginalized clients are able to find institutional systems that support their core beliefs, whatever these may be, they are "empowered," and empowerment lifts depression, provides emotional focus, and reduces loneliness. On the negative side, no matter what a therapist may think of a client's belief system, the possibility of changing that belief system in a significant way is probably remote.

Boundaries

Explanations of diversity and synergy lead us to consider the ways in which we define and maintain our own separate belief systems and our sense of ourselves, individually or collectively. Why do certain kinds of clothes or certain kinds of activities absolutely not feel like "me"? Why do we refer to certain behaviors or beliefs as "un-American"? The explanation is that these are system boundary definitions, and we are all differentiated at our boundaries—the place where your personality ends and mine begins, where I end and the material world begins, or where my institution ends and a different one begins.

Every system desperately tries to maintain its boundaries. Boundary protection may take the form of arguments, wars, nationalism, psychological narcissism, dogmatism (in churches and elsewhere), and even, sometimes, psychosis. Without a solid sense of differentiated self, a person will literally begin to feel crazy, and without clear and distinguishable boundaries, a larger system will cease to exist. So boundary protection is essential to system maintenance. How paradoxical it is that we sometimes require brutal systems of boundary preservation so that separate entities can exist in the world. Ken Wilbur (1979) has written a thought-provoking book about the ways in which boundary maintenance creates evil in the world, and yet, as he points out, without systems of self-preservation, there could be no life on earth of any kind.

The boundary dilemma explains some of our professional controversies. Why are we so passionate in our defense of whatever we believe in, whether a therapeutic method, a social norm, or a political assumption? Why do we feel we should "educate" everyone into whatever seems to be the "best" way of doing whatever it is we do? In our personal lives, why are people who differ from ourselves in skin color, customs, or values so distasteful to us for no logical reason? (I am always shocked to hear small children make fun of someone who seems unusual.) The reason may be that differences feel dangerous, threatening to invade our psychological borders and overwhelm us with ideas and values at odds with our own.

As we have noted, boundary maintenance is the primary task of all living organisms. And a principal way in which self-aware creatures such as ourselves maintain our psychological boundaries is through the imaginative syndromes that we call belief systems. In our mental health practices, we can enhance our essential sense of separate self by enhancing the beliefs by which we define ourselves.

Most systems function best with flexible boundaries that can shut out encroachments that threaten their integrity but be open to external influences that will promote growth and health. Gestalt therapists Erv and Miriam Polster (1973) use the expression "working at the boundary," meaning the actual place in space and time where we encounter each other via our sense organs, and they offer excellent therapeutic techniques for respecting or modifying psychological boundaries.

As an extreme example of inflexible boundary protection, I think of Betty, a client whose basic premise about reality was that the world is a hostile place and that personal alertness and willingness to "get even" are fundamental to safety. Every sentence out of my mouth was a potential challenge to her boundaries. "What do you mean by that?" she would counter if I said something even as benign as "You're right on time" or "You look very cheery today." She was a fortress, surrounded by moats, protected by sharpshooters. She had an uncanny way of evaluating insults to gauge the level of getting even that was required, and she took great satisfaction in "getting them where it hurts."

On the surface this looked like paranoia of the most flagrant kind. But there were no gaps in Betty's defensiveness; it had a supremely consistent quality, and finally I began to see some patterns emerging. I learned that she had grown up in West Virginia, literally on a creek in the mountains. She was part of a culture that had been more or less isolated from the rest of society for many generations and had come to the Midwest to attend college on a scholarship earmarked for Appalachian students.

"Getting even seems to be very important to you," I finally thought to observe to her, and I discovered she was astonished by the notion that getting even was not important to all of us in her new environment. Where she came from, everyone "kept score," and the core beliefs of the entire culture revolved around who was ahead, grudgewise. Because the latest recipient of her scorekeeping was her new fiancé, who was getting fed up with the whole business, we carefully tiptoed around her beliefs to see if we could find some way for her to feel safe and still let down her guard occasionally.

Belief systems have odd boundaries, not predictable by normal rational inquiry. At one time I suppose it was reasonable to stand at the door of an Appalachian cabin with rifle ready, alert to see if it was friend or foe coming over the next ridge. And just as national honor requires bombing raids to prove that we cannot be taken advantage of, psychological honor in a belief system such as Betty's required retributive raids to warn potential enemies that boundaries were not to be tampered with. But the physical threat had long since disappeared; only the belief system remained.

All this is also of interest in assessing the rules and dogmas of the belief systems to which our clients subscribe. For example, what appear to be inflexible personal boundaries to an outsider—rules, expectations, penalties—may be extremely important for system maintenance if an individual or an organization is somewhat fragile or if it is under assault from the external society, and likewise, rigid institutional boundaries are frequently useful to individuals who are in need of stern external structures to keep them from falling apart. (This may be one reason why military service is so attractive to many people and why going back to prison is not necessarily the punishment for some people that it would be for most.) To the frequent dismay of their professional therapists, clients in need of external boundaries may be attracted to harsh, fundamen-

talist sects, either religious or political, with clear, tough expectations (think of the "skinheads" as a secular example) as a way to
find external meaning when internal meaning is absent.

Mental health professionals have for many years been sensitive
to the need to shore up the delicate psychological margins of their
most vulnerable clients by enhancing their sense of self. I am arguing here that among the most important sources of self-definition
are the irrational collections of assumptions we make about life,
our core beliefs, and we should not be surprised when needy clients
find self-definitions in powerful cults or totalitarian institutions.

Summary

Human belief systems have inevitable and intractable characteristics that no amount of exasperation can modify. They are inevitably
diverse, driven by synergistic energies, and defined by boundaries
that will not succumb to reductionist analysis. Human beings order
experience within belief systems and (sometimes unfortunately)
defend those beliefs with their lives, fortunes, and sacred honor.

Chapter Four

Structures of Religious Beliefs

Several of what I am calling *structures* of belief systems are peculiar to religious belief systems. Recognize that a religious belief system is not a religious institution. A religious institution comprises many belief systems. In fact, as I will point out later, many church members do not even believe in a conventional idea of God. In this discussion, *religion* will refer to any belief system imputing a definition of universal meaning to human life, usually, *but not always*, implying some sort of deity.

Religious belief systems serve two distinct purposes. As do all belief systems, they define reality, but out of their definitions of reality comes moral awareness—an intimation that life has direction and purpose. As will become apparent, it is this moral awareness that particularly sets them apart. (The "rules" imposed by religious institutions grow out of this moral awareness and vary widely from culture to culture. *Morality* and *commandments* are not synonymous.) As you can see, we are returning to square one—what is real, what is good? It is not possible to take seriously a client's most private and powerful set of core beliefs without asking those two questions. But unless we are satisfied with superficial answers, we need to examine again the sources of our sense of the "real" and the "good."

We begin this exploration of religious beliefs by observing that our concepts of what is real evolve out of the interaction between our subjective experience and the external "things" in the world— the interaction, in other words, between thoughts and sensations. We will consider how our interior and exterior experiences are related, and how our mental constructs in some sense create the different things in our environment—sometimes called the "subject-object split."

Out of this subjective experience of external reality comes the observation that reality seems to consist of sets of opposites: good–bad, up–down, hard–soft, light–dark, and so forth. I will be referring to these as "dualities" and will base my argument about moral origins on the suggestion that dualities—material and ethical polarities—are essential to meaning and especially to our concepts of good and evil. (Stop and think about this for a moment. How would you know if something was soft if you did not have a mental image of hardness? How would you know light if you had never experienced darkness? What meaning would goodness have for you if you had never confronted evil?)

Bear with me and take this next discussion slowly. This sort of philosophical speculation may seem so abstract as to be incomprehensible, but it is my conviction that by understanding the importance of the difference between subjective and objective experience, we can begin to understand what we mean by the word *real*, and by clarifying our understanding of good and evil, we can begin to understand the moral dilemmas of some of our clients.

The Subject-Object Split

No question is more fundamental to both religion and psychology than the relationship of self to other, whether other people or Wholly Other. As we have suggested, a premise of our culture is that we are each separate beings with connections only at our boundaries. When in imagination and dreams we experience the ghostly presence of others, that is held to be a manifestation of our own minds, and in no way is it seen as communication. Extrasensory perception may hold a certain titillating fascination for many of us, but it has no place in scientific encounters or precepts. Experiences that do not fit into our concept of ourselves as conscious "objects"—synchronicities, telepathy, precognitions, and the like—are explained away as coincidences or misunderstandings or are dismissed as irrelevant.

Yet if we are to take prayer seriously or to believe in the idea of "leadings," of motivation originating elsewhere than in our own psyche, then the notion of persons as objects not essentially different from trees and stones and computers except for a coincidental chemical anomaly called consciousness must somehow be modified. Otherwise, all the acceptance in the world of pluralities, of differences, of complexities will lead only to amused tolerance on the part of mental health professionals when they encounter that most basic religious belief, that there is an interaction with a force unexplainable in scientific or mechanical terms that makes it possible for us to influence reality with our prayers.

I contend that the human being is neither an object in a world of objects nor a set of ideas in a world of illusions but is in some sense both. This is a puzzling idea to get hold of, but it is central to the rationale I am trying to develop. What we perceive to be real very largely depends on the relationship between our subjective constructs and our objective experience.

I once conducted an informal survey of friends concerning their concepts of reality. To stimulate ideas, I devised a written set of possible responses, such as "Reality is less than it seems and is probably reducible to a single simple explanation," "Reality is more than it seems and is probably beyond human understanding," and "There are many realities." As we discussed our reactions to these propositions, it became clear that I had caught myself in the very trap I had been striving to avoid—I had thought of reality as something "out there." But my friends responded to my questions in more subjective ways, personally and unscientifically. I confess that initially I felt irritated. They seemed to have missed the point of the discussion. They were saying things like "Things I thought real when I was twelve no longer seemed real when I was twenty-five" and "Reality is one thing for a snail and another for a whale." But upon reflection, I realized that they were right. How we experience the world depends entirely on our perspective, which changes as we change. As living creatures, and especially as human beings, we are not merely thinking objects in a world of material objects. Our consciousness and imagination give us the peculiar quality we call *sub-*

jectivity; humans are, above all, self-reflective creatures engaged in the continuous process of creating themselves.

In spite of our commonsense impressions, reality is not "discovered" by reason alone; there are not absolute patterns "out there," independent of ourselves, that we can decipher with logic, nor, conversely, is truth merely a subjective idea with no corollary in the objective world. Rather we construct truth as we go along; the ongoing interaction between our subjective experience and the external world in some mysterious way results in what we perceive as real.

I am not saying that reality consists only of what we wish it to be. I contend, of course, that there *is* something "out there." Most helpful to me in understanding this philosophy is to assume myself blind from birth and then imagine what it would be like suddenly to gain the capacity to see. Until that moment, all my experiences would be tied to my senses of taste, smell, hearing, and, especially, touch. For example, my sense of "chair" would derive from the pressure I felt when I sat down on a chair or what the chair felt like when I explored it with my hands or feet. But if I were suddenly able to see, I would at first, presumably, be flooded with a chaos of light and shapes that would have no meaning. Only as I began to relate the light patterns to the pressure patterns previously experienced by my muscles and skin would the image of a chair have any meaning at all to me. There is, it seems, no absolute "chair." A butterfly would conceive of a chair differently from a blind person, and a porpoise would experience it differently still, should a chair ever go floating by.

Our scientific background has taught us to validate ideas with objective evidence. "Be behaviorally specific," I used to tell my social work students when they made assertions about clients, and for many years the world of psychology tried sternly to be scientific out of our sense that if something can be observed, it is real. The real seems to be the external, and yet—in our most successful practices we build our therapies around our inner lives. Most therapists are fascinated with dreams (both waking and sleeping), and surely these are the most subjective possible experiences. We do not perceive them to be, as some skeptic has put it, "mental garbage." For practical reasons, we are willing to consider dreams to be real. Yet oddly enough, we do not take the next small step and move from fascination with dreams to fascination with prayers. In my own practice, and even considering that I would presume myself to be sensitive to anyone's prayer life, I cannot remember a single instance of a client sharing the content of prayers with me in any detail. Nor do I recall sharing with my therapists more than passing allusions to my own prayers. I suspect that more than most social scientists, mental health people are sympathetic to the importance of subjective experience. So I can only suppose that it is the nature of psychological belief systems, excluding prayers from therapy in what I can only call a prejudicial way, that creates such a puzzling blind spot.

This, then, becomes another illustration of the somewhat irrational nature of our belief systems. The frameworks they provide are built from inner and outer realities that are functional for each of us as individuals and do not succumb to the logic of rational inquiry. When we professionals are tempted to discount someone's beliefs as being "unrealistic," it behooves us to consider how that person's subjective experience differs from our own and how our own represents the sum of the interaction between the objective events of our lives and the subjective interpretations that organize and make sense of them.

Unity Versus Duality

The relationship between subjective and objective experience could be thought of as an illustration of duality. The word *duality* has had several meanings in the history of philosophy, most often referring to the separation of soul and body. I would like to use the word in a slightly different way, however. In this discussion, I will be using it in opposition to the word *unity*, to indicate the existence of "particularities," or separate "things" (with the associated characteristic of implying their opposites) in the universe. This concept is crucial to our discussion because it suggests the reasons for our disagreements about the existence of good and evil.

Mental health professionals have tended unquestioningly to accept ideas of good and evil as situationally relative. Maybe stealing is evil, but not if my children are starving. Maybe adultery is evil, but not if I am the victim of a loveless marriage, starved for affection and sexual expression. But most religious belief systems assert that good and evil are absolutes, perhaps interpreted situationally but with intrinsic meaning outside our individual dilemmas. This assertion is, I think, often difficult for professionals to accept. By considering the fundamental nature of duality, as we understand it, I hope to present one possible way to find an intellectual justification for religious moral systems.

Let me indulge in a little theology here. The word *duality* is sometimes regarded as though it were a totalitarian plot rather than describing, as it does, the original source of meaning in the world. I want to stress that without the differentiation of separate entities, there would be no Creation in the biblical sense. Let me repeat this for emphasis. Until reality became more than just an undifferentiated blob of amorphous nothing, no things could exist, and without things, there would no meaning. That is what mythical creation stories are all about. In our Jewish and Christian Bibles, after God created light, He proceeded to create specificities of all kinds. The naming that He is then alleged to have engaged in is a mythical way of suggesting that meaning had come into the world.

I am always puzzled that it is not self-evident that unless there were particularities—birds and bees and trees and you and me—there would be no systems of thought, no beauty, no meaning in any sense in which we use the words. It is, then, fundamentally true that the first necessity for experience and for philosophizing about experience is what we are calling duality, which allows for the evolution of progressive differentiations. Duality, as the creation of separate entities, has, by definition, sets of opposites. And, to repeat, good and evil are unavoidable opposites; we cannot experience goodness without a corresponding understanding of badness; the one concept has no meaning without the other.

This does not mean that because it is unavoidable, evil should be discounted. It only means that we must take polar opposites seriously and acknowledge that the ultimately decisive response that human beings can make to duality is the moral response: the response of good versus evil. In all cultures, religions have typically addressed the inevitability of evil. So it is important to stress that moral judgments are not merely annoyances or outmoded irrelevancies; they are central to a particular understanding of reality. In our appreciation of duality, it is important to maintain our powers of discernment of good and evil.

But to get back to Creation, the world religions have always believed that our dualities emerged from a central unity. And whether or not we call it God, religion has always alleged it is possible to experience that unity. The psychiatrist Gerald May (1982) points out that we have all had the experience of unity for a brief instant when we are utterly absorbed in some activity or experience—watching a sunset, creating a piece of art, encountering a loved person—when, fleetingly, all comparisons, ambitions, grudges, and doubts vanish into the transcendent moment. The ability to escape from preoccupation with self and to live in continual awareness of life's larger context is a goal of most of the advanced religions—presented and conceptualized as prayer without ceasing, meditation, contemplation of sacred objects, living the monastic life, or in some other way. Many methods and disciplines lead to an outcome of unity.

The confusion within the mental health world over the question of unity versus duality (though not phrased this way at the time) can be illustrated by the confusion occurring when Transcendental Meditation (TM) first became popular, concurrent with the psychological fallout from the early experiments with psychedelic drugs. There was great concern at that time within mental health circles that if individuals loosened their mental grip on reality—allowed their boundaries to dissolve through drugs or meditation—among other dangerous results, the ego would weaken, permitting primitive impulses to surge to the surface, causing outbreaks of psychosis. There was an assumption that strong ego boundaries depended on remaining in excellent touch with "reality." (A case should be made for the reverse: that good reality testing results from a strong ego.) But the introduction of various kinds of meditation, Eastern religions like Zen Buddhism, and the counterculture use of mind-altering chemicals created experiences of what seemed to be some sort of universal awareness, and interest in philosophies stressing the unity of creation suggested to many serious thinkers that our seeming separateness was an illusion and that experiences of unity could, in fact, enhance our mental health. Indeed, meditation and its cousins hypnosis and relaxation have become common techniques in many psychotherapeutic arsenals.

The existential experience of unity attracts me, as I presume it attracts many people, as a longed-for ideal: to be able to confront painful illness, death, war, ugliness, and cruelty with equanimity, knowing that all these are illusions and that we are indestructible parts of a larger whole. Popular mythology has described ways in which a few lucky people have apparently achieved this goal under odd circumstances such as a near-death experience or a sudden religious conversion, but even though we have reports of modern-day mystics who live in this rarified realm (the open, gracious, amused face of the Dalai Lama immediately comes to my mind), ordinary experience seems to demonstrate that most of us are stuck in our thorny, impassioned, self-absorbed worlds and that somehow we have to make the best of it.

Because unity and duality are both real, the question for mental health professionals becomes not which idea is true but which idea is most helpful in the living of an individual life or, to be more precise, which reality is available to the individual at any given time. To be true to my premises, I will argue that there is room for both.

Summary

A belief system can be considered religious to the extent that it not only defines reality but also offers moral absolutes growing out of its reality definition. (By "moral absolute," I do not mean rules governing behavior. I mean, rather, the existential goal toward which the living of one's life is directed.) Definitions of reality result from the subjective interpretation of objective stimuli, the things in the universe that give meaning to creation. But because the existence of things implies what we are calling *duality*—sets of opposites— we must inevitably confront moral dilemmas, because goodness is inextricably bound to its opposite, evil, and cannot be wished away by considerations of psychological relativism.

There are two principal ways of relating to good and evil: through the discernment of these moral opposites in myths and codes of behavior (as happens in "dualistic" religious systems, most notably our three Western religions, Judaism, Christianity, and Islam) or through subjective return to the unity from which things originated (especially in religious practices growing out of Eastern religions, most notably Hinduism and Buddhism).

Chapter Five

Acknowledging Alternative Beliefs

Mr. and Mrs. W., a couple in their late forties, had come to see me for marital counseling. During the course of taking their history, I learned that they had at one time been "swingers"—they had engaged in sexual mate-swapping with other married couples—but this had been many years earlier, and they did not present it as relevant to their current serious misunderstandings. However, Mr. W.'s occasional sexual affairs since that time had finally caused his wife's patience to run out. "I realized," she said bitterly, "that I was sick of wondering who he was sleeping with. I just didn't want to be part of that scene anymore, and I thought it was time he grew up." As might be expected, Mr. W. was insulted and felt stifled by his wife's midlife conventionality and unwillingness to take risks. "She knew what she was getting when she married me," he remarked with annoyance. "She's the one who changed, not me."

At first glance, this situation seemed fairly straightforward, but when I asked the W.'s about their "gut feelings" about life, it soon became apparent that in this area they were very different from each other. "You know," Mrs. W. explained, "when we first met, I was still a teenager. I suppose I was rebelling against my family, and because we were both were very much against the Vietnam War, it seemed as though we had a lot in common. But our own kids are growing up now, and I've started to believe that my parents weren't so wrong after all. I don't think I want the kids following our example."

I could see Mr. W. roll his eyes; he had heard this before. "Oh yeah?" he asked her sarcastically. "I'm such a terrible person? Is that what you tell them?"

Not wanting to listen to a rerun of an old scenario, I shifted direction. "Tell me," I asked them, "what do you each hope to get out of life? What do you think life is all about?"

At first the W.'s did not understand what I was getting at, but after I suggested a few alternatives (maybe life isn't about anything, or maybe life experiences are tests of our character), Mrs. W. grew thoughtful. "I think life is a sort of classroom," she said. She looked embarrassed and glanced at her husband. "For our souls," she added hesitantly.

Mr. W. stared at her. "For your soul? You believe in souls?"

"You don't?" I asked him.

"No, I certainly don't. What's a 'soul'? That's stupid. We're alive and then someday we're dead and that's all there is to it. So while you're alive, you might as well do all the things you want to do. If I live to be seventy-five, I don't want to kick myself for having missed out on something." There was perplexity in his expression as he looked at his wife. "I thought you felt that way too."

At my instigation, the W.'s then had a long and more or less amiable conversation about the differences in their beliefs about life: where they originated, how and why they had changed, and what the implications were for other areas of their lives. It became apparent that these differences would not be easy to resolve, and in fact, a short time later the W.'s separated.

The W.'s situation illustrates the ways in which our core beliefs about what is real and good directly influence our behavior and our relationships. The nature of reality and the dilemma of ethics are the crucial questions in any individual's belief system, and as we have been suggesting, these can vary greatly and still have internal coherence and logic. I would like in this chapter to review some overarching ideas that may explain the origins of belief systems such as these and raise some questions that remain unanswered. These are huge arenas of intellectual thought that take us unavoidably into philosophy, and I do not pretend to do more than open the door on them.

Alternative Views of Reality

Many years ago, the psychologist-philosopher William James ([1902] 1958) delivered a series of lectures in Edinburgh, Scotland, on the subject of the psychology of the religious impulse. In these now-famous Gifford lectures, he discussed in great detail such subjects as mysticism, saintliness, conversion, repentance, reward, and punishment. He carefully tried to avoid a partisan stance, but in the end he acknowledged his belief that "the world of our present consciousness is only one out of many worlds of consciousness that exist, and that those other worlds must contain experiences which have a meaning for our life also" (p. 42). He pointed out that because we all live in the universe, we cannot avoid making assumptions about it. "For when all is said and done, we are in the end absolutely dependent on the universe; and into sacrifices and surrenders of some sort, deliberately looked at and accepted, we are drawn and pressed as into our only permanent positions of repose" (p. 56).

As James understood nearly a century ago, and as has been demonstrated repeatedly by scientists and philosophers since then, materialism and current scientific knowledge do not provide adequate explanations of our existence. Yet psychology has tended to proceed from the assumption, not only that there is just one commonsense view of reality, but also that persons in need of psychological treatment can be presumed to subscribe to that view and, worse yet, that if they do not, their deviance presents an additional symptom for treatment.

But the commonsense view is beginning to be questioned in many quarters. Lawrence LeShan (1976) and more recently Richard Broughton (1991) have argued that mystical states, clairvoyant experiences, and modern physics all seem to demonstrate realities different from the ordinary. LeShan notes that everyday experience—"conventional reality"—is reductionistic and linear. As a consequence, we have assumed for several centuries that the whole can be understood by examining its parts and that for every effect there is a cause. But as we discussed earlier, complex systems do not lend themselves to reductionistic explanations, and furthermore, we are beginning to suspect that once something is part of a whole, it is always part of that whole, even if the parts are no longer connected in space and time—a truly revolutionary thought. This is one of the mysterious implications of recent discoveries in particle physics, and though lay extrapolations of this kind may annoy traditional scientists, any number of thinkers have flirted with these ideas.

It may be that time, space, matter, and energy (all of which are variations of the same thing) are simply convenient ways of thinking about reality and that, mind-boggling as it is to consider, there may also be modes of reality outside of space and time without cause-and-effect parameters. LeShan argues that the apparent contradictions between conventional reality and "clairvoyant reality" are illusory, perhaps extreme points on a reality continuum. He suggests that we need conventional reality for our everyday life and clairvoyant reality to understand exceptional events, not only in physics, where a new theory is needed to deal with effects that seem to have no perceptual correlates, but also in paranormal psychology, where we have tended to dismiss as impossible a vast body of substantiated data because it contradicts conventional scientific wisdom. In fact, Broughton points out that no matter how carefully constructed experiments in paranormal psychology may be, because they are outside the belief systems of most scientists (the "paradigms" within which they operate), they *cannot* be accepted by conventional science without causing a significant shift in the paradigm.

Because of the magnitude and controversial nature of this subject and because a number of writers have in fact suggested that we are on the verge of just such a paradigm shift, I would like to highlight a few books that I find especially informative and provocative. The English science writer Bryan Appleyard's controversial book *Understanding the Present* (1992), about the ways in which scientific thinking has undermined our ethical base, and Duke Uni-

versity professor Richard Broughton's careful review of current scientific findings in the world of paranormal psychology in his book
Parapsychology (1991) are particularly interesting. The physicist
Freeman Dyson has also addressed the dangers of reductionism in
a way that opens the door on new intellectual possibilities in his
fascinating book *Infinite in All Directions* (1988), and the scientist
Fritjof Capra has written several books about new scientific paradigms, including *The Turning Point* (1983) and, with theologian
David Stendl-Rast, *Belonging to the Universe* (1992).

Alternative Views of Ethics

We have already noted that a major stumbling block in working
with beliefs other than our own is the subconscious sense that a different belief is "bad." Not only have mental health professionals
tended to accept conventional wisdom about reality, but they have
also somewhat unquestioningly accepted a pragmatic view of
ethics: "goodness" is whatever "works" rather than an absolute
value. And although the professional norm has long been that we
work with "what is" rather than "what ought to be," our reactions
to our clients' lives are never entirely neutral.

Historically, the nature of goodness and evil has been a particular struggle between religion and science (including mental
health), and the complex nature of human ethics has been a source
of bitter conflict. For centuries, organized religion initially repressed
and finally responded to assertions raised by the scientific method
that values are relative. (The Roman Catholic Church has only
recently abandoned its opposition to "modernism," the scientific
method that insists on proof and is skeptical of anything suggesting superstition.) A theological reason for this conflict is that in
Judeo-Christian thought, something that substitutes for God, as
scientific methodology has tended to do, is held to be intrinsically
evil.

Also, science has contended that possibilities must be held
open, and there is always more to discover. Therefore, to believe
in absolutes, as religions do, contradicts one of the fundamental

premises of scientific belief systems and undermines the scientific enterprise by closing off large areas of exploration. However, some modern scientists have also been theologians—Pierre Teilhard de Chardin comes to mind—and many people have observed that there need not be anything inherently antagonistic between religion and science. As noted earlier, this is becoming more and more true as religious studies become more scientific and science becomes more philosophical.

But how are we then to decide what is good or bad? The theologian Hans Kung, in a lecture at the University of Michigan in 1985, suggested that the familiar argument that good and evil are only relative, depending on the context in which they occur, is sophistry. He observed that we do in fact recognize good and evil when we encounter them; no mentally healthy person argues that the Holocaust was a good thing, and very few people would find evil in Mother Teresa of Calcutta. Kung noted that there are a few common human values on which a majority of humankind agrees and that in fact these were spelled out in the original Universal Declaration of Human Rights. For example, no moral person wants to exterminate the human race: murder (not necessarily killing, as our frequent wars demonstrate) is fairly universally condemned, as are many practices that jeopardize health and human dignity.

But in addition, Kung suggests that ethical belief systems can be considered both horizontally and vertically: horizontally in the sense of our relationships with each other and vertically in considering our individual relationship with the absolute. Surveying the horizontal dimension, Kung argues that the catastrophic consequences of the proposition that there is only one "true religion"— a proposition of which all major belief systems, both religious and secular, have been guilty—should by now cause us to question its validity. But thinking vertically, each person, living an individual life, *has* to subscribe to a particular belief system; one cannot believe all kinds of contradictory propositions at the same time. However—and this is a major qualifier—*within each belief system are both good and evil.* Kung reminds us that we are all in process, working out life as we go along, and one of our primary tasks seems to be to increase the amount of goodness in the world. Nothing is yet fin-ished: not our planet, our individual lives, our knowledge, or even our religions, however much we may behave as if we alone have immutable pipelines to the Divine.

The Nature of the Human Being

Just as our belief systems are based on philosophical concepts of reality and ethics, so also are they based on anthropology, and in addition to exploring beliefs about reality, we need to explore beliefs—and *belief*, I will argue, is the accurate word—about the nature of the human being: who we are, what our place is in the universe, what we should hope for in our individual lives. In the next several chapters we will examine a variety of core belief sys-tems—secular, religious, and psychological—that differ in their views of human nature. I will suggest why I think everyone has a conscious or an unconscious view of the human being's role in the universe and why it is therefore imperative for mental health pro-fessionals to be both open-minded in their assessments and their treatment approaches and sensitive to their own biases.

The drama professor Arthur Little titled his Earlham College baccalaureate address "Living As If," from which I have borrowed the title of this book. He talked about the suspension of disbelief that is necessary for enjoyment of drama—indeed, for any of the arts—and then extended this idea to life itself. He reminded us that while we are absorbed in a play, we are in fact living as if the play were true. He suggested that we all do this in everyday life and that to some extent we choose our own life dramas but that whether we choose them or not, we unconsciously live as if certain absolutes were true.

Are we speaking here of premises? Something more poetic and personal is meant than the word *premise* suggests. Little meant that sometimes we simply have to live as if it matters that we love peo-ple or that we can effect change in the world or that good will ulti-mately triumph, even when we have doubts or understand that there may be no scientific validation for our assumptions. We may not be able to prove that those things are so, but our lives are more beautiful and more meaningful if we speak sternly to our skeptical selves and plunge ahead in fearless faith. He meant that when we do this, to some extent we create a new reality with our lives, just as the artist creates an entirely new reality with imagination and skill.

In developing the theme of this discussion, I would like to walk around inside a number of life stances—"as ifs"—to see how one might behave and feel and think if one proceeded from them. It seems to me that a basic flaw in most counseling and therapeutic encounters is the assumption that the therapist's and the client's as ifs are the same, and I think until we understand the implications of different viewpoints, we will continually tend to fly at different altitudes and to wonder why we fail to connect.

Core beliefs are central to individual lives, and they are also central to larger systems such as professions and institutions. Persons live as if certain absolutes were true, and collective ideologies do the same, though the assumptions of collective systems, even more than those of individuals, tend to be hidden or not articulated. Personal belief systems can be divided somewhat arbitrarily into the religious (which assume that life has existential meaning) and the secular. Collective systems could include professions of all sorts and even certain political systems, but because this discussion is directed to mental health practitioners, I am interested primarily in the beliefs that undergird mental health theories. The next three chapters outline some common as ifs as they apply to secular, religious, and psychological core beliefs and suggest some life questions appropriate to each. In Chapter Ten we will attempt to match treatment approaches with these existential assumptions.

I would like to reflect for a moment on the observation made earlier that there are striking similarities between personal belief systems and psychological ones. The problems of trying to capture the human psyche inside conceptual models are in many ways microcosms of the problems of trying to think about God and reality. Just as reality itself is continually in process and even being created by ourselves as observers, so too we human beings are in process and being created by our very attempts to study and treat ourselves. And just as all religions have somehow to deal with both body and spirit, even if by denying one or the other, so too psychology is confronted with the human person as both body and mind (spirit, consciousness). We are bounded and not bounded, observable and mysterious, determined and free. Furthermore, religion and psychology must each simultaneously deal with both individual persons and communities or institutions.

Religious wars, overt and armed or covert and political, have stemmed from arrogant and rigidly doctrinaire assumptions. The exact same statement could be made about therapeutic wars, excepting only that the arsenals of warfare are words and money and reputations. It has often seemed to me that the antipathy between the religious community and psychology has a strong element of projection. Intolerance and dogmatism are familiar, if frequently denied, in both places. Many pastors view the psychological community's competing claims of efficacy with confusion, at the same time that they are being told by psychologists to leave clinical matters to the clinicians. Many psychologists discount the insights of religion, and the fractured world of organized religion can rarely summon a unified enough voice with which to reply. Though practitioners may subscribe to differing points of view, there are implications in each point of reference for the believer and for the mental health professional.

Dialogue is possible only when commonalities have been established between all of our various life stances, our as ifs. We must be able to understand at a deep level that we are more alike than we are different. We will discuss in greater detail in Chapter Nine the two commonalities that most traditional mental health systems share with each other and with traditional belief systems. The first of these is the emphasis on the curative and fundamental importance of love or, as psychology has tended to call it, "relationship." The second is the importance of metaphor and other symbolic representations of reality in our understanding of human nature and the universe.

Summary

Ideally, as mental health professionals, we do not insist that our clients share our sexual orientations or our political beliefs or our life-styles. Perhaps the time has come to recognize that they frequently do not share our belief systems either and that we enhance our encounters together when we share and respect the varieties of our experience. We can tune in to the individual life questions of our clients if we walk lovingly around inside the answers that their particular metaphors provide, acknowledging to ourselves that we also have our own need to explain reality and our own metaphorical universes.

Chapter Six

⚊

Secular As Ifs

The word secular usually implies "of this world," but that is not quite how I want to use it here. I am suggesting that belief systems not having a concept of God be differentiated from those that do, but this does not mean that the following core beliefs are necessarily free of metaphysical conclusions and are solely "scientific." I will begin with atheism, which is clearly secular, but I will also include humanism, which sometimes spills over into religion, and what I am calling the "search for unity," which is reflected not only in New Age spirituality (as I understand it, a combination of mysticism and ethnic religious practices) but also in most of the world's religions in some form or other. So *secular* in this chapter means primarily "not ordained by God" but does not necessarily exclude the metaphysical.

I want to suggest in this presentation that our core beliefs raise questions our lives seem *impelled* to answer—answering them may happen unconsciously, as was the case with the W.'s, but it is never optional—and these questions underlie all mental health practice. So to the extent we can excavate someone's underlying beliefs, we can address that individual's life questions in a meaningful way. Sam Keen says of this universal need to find meaning in life:

> Metaphysics and myth-making are a game of making a whole out of parts, a way of teasing the fragments of life into a vision of completeness. To play the game, we take some important aspect of human experience and let the imagination run wild. Let's suppose the world is like a big animal, or a plant, or a city, or an artifact, or a business, or a . . . dream, or a machine, . . . or a love relationship.

Everybody plays the game, consciously or unconsciously. There is no way not to play it. . . . This is our each and only world: Every person must wager a single life on power, or knowledge, or love, or work, or conquest, or comfort, or adventure, or on some god of clan [1983, p. 15].

Keen is saying in metaphorical language what we said earlier about the nature of existence: no one knows what reality is, but ignorance does not absolve us of the necessity of accepting some set of existential ideas that makes sense to us.

Atheism

Suppose we live as if there is no such thing as God. What we perceive to be real, or what we can detect experimentally, is the totality of all there is. It is true that we have not exhausted the possibilities of science and that many questions remain unanswered, but that is because we haven't answered them *yet*, not because they are unanswerable. Furthermore, reality is basically simple. The scientific task is to discover an underlying principle that will explain all of the seeming complexities. Notions of good and bad are relative. They exist in the environment of the definer rather than as abstract absolutes. There is no "direction" to evolution in any supernatural sense, except that provided by observable natural phenomena. Nor is there any "meaning" to human life, and we assume that anthropomorphism is responsible for the concept of God. Furthermore, human consciousness, which at some level seems so wonderful, is merely an odd aberration that will eventually be explained by the laws of science and is probably merely another chance event in a meaningless universe of matter and energy.

If we are to be consistent, the basic moral principle is self-interest: what is good for me will be good for you. Altruism is not only self-delusionary but also ultimately destructive. Although this may seem to advocate the law of the jungle, human reason will usually outwit brute strength, and the human animal seems to have the capacity for loving relationships. So the goal of life is not only to follow Machiavelli along the paths of canniness but also to find pleasure through living caringly, resourcefully, and energetically. The weak will no doubt sometimes fall by the wayside, but evolution teaches us that the survival of our species, like all others, depends on natural selection. Anyway, the human imagination is such that we cannot be comfortable with absolute ruthlessness. It will occur to us that common decency contributes to our own well-being and that of others. But happiness is the obvious goal of human life because we get no second chance and there is no higher authority to which we are accountable. We get what we can.

The basic life question of atheists has been asked since the Enlightenment, and Thomas Jefferson later managed to imply it in the Declaration of Independence: *How can we be happy?* Happiness, whatever it is, is the goal of life, and since we only get this one life, pursuing happiness will be our primary preoccupation. When I was a secular therapist, I did not feel ethically justified in questioning the unremitting and desperate longing for happiness that my clients presented to me. I am sometimes tempted by it in my personal life as well, and I wonder if there is anyone who is not. "How can I be happy?" has an appealing innocence in its phraseology and a potential snare in its actualization. Culturally, in our era we seem to be playing out the implications of the search for happiness without ethical restraints. As a therapist, I am concerned to know whether my client has an existential sense of responsibility or lives in a meaningless world in which the cleverest and most ruthless survive. In its extreme version, we see it as sociopathy or psychopathy, but cheaters (in marriage, business, or government) who rationalize their behavior out of a sense of getting what they can out of their one and only life are no less influenced by this philosophy.

I think this stance is more common than is publicly acknowledged not only among therapists but also among church people, even among clergy. Church membership is by no means a guarantee of belief in God. That atheism is the core belief of some members of congregations first occurred to me when I attempted to discuss "faith" with an older member of a Lutheran church and kept running into dead ends. Questions and leads elicited no response. Suddenly I realized that she didn't have anything to say about God because she didn't believe in God. She was a lifelong Lutheran in her late seventies. The church was her socioemotional base. My hunch is that she paid lip service to a set of beliefs she had abandoned when she was young—if, indeed, they were ever there—but that the church community was so important to her that it would have been unthinkable to say out loud that she thought the whole thing was basically nonsense. In addition, I am convinced that some of the dissonance between ministers and congregations is created by the closet atheism of some ministers. How many ministers have said to themselves, if not to others (as one did, in fact, say to me), "Those people are too religious for me!"

The problem with an unrelenting search for happiness comes when inevitable trouble occurs. That one can win all of life's various games if one is canny enough is often the wonderful assumption of the wealthy, white American. ("In good health," whispers a mean little voice.) When the stock market then collapses, this grown-up child jumps out the window of a tall building. The existential complaint is, *It's not fair!*

Humanism

Suppose we live as if common sense should prevail. We assume that reality is too complex ever to understand completely, but we assume that if we follow the rules that have been laid down over the centuries by our forebears and our governments, we will have the benefit of prior generations of experience. Ultimate reality seems basically benevolent, but in any case it seems not to interfere in the operation of creation. This view derives from Descartes and the Enlightenment and is still the subtle philosophical horizon of most of modern European civilization. It is also the underlying assumption of most of Western education.

We are here assuming that the customs and rituals of religion are psychological, artistic, and historic observances, valuable and even essential to mental and social health but without mystical meaning. Any suggestion of the supernatural implies a belief in magic and is not only contrary to scientific method but also directly responsible for many of the world's evils. In this Cartesian world, knowledge is the key to freedom and progress, and superstition and magic are enemies of knowledge. Acknowledged or not, this is the life stance not only of the secular Western world but also of many of the liberal religions.

If a deity does not interfere with material reality (perhaps we are willing to concede a "Ground of Being," which is more personal than the philosophers' Great Watchmaker but a benevolent non-intervener nonetheless), then *what we do is supremely important.* Talk is cheap. Progress is up to all of us, and when we fail to act, we create the hells—wars, holocausts, hatred—with which we have been stuck. Social benevolence—the greatest good for the greatest number—is the ethic by which we live righteous and moral lives. We believe that goodness matters, and the understanding that we have to take care of ourselves causes us to study and educate and nurture humankind for the sake of us all because there will be no miracles to bail us out when the human ship starts to go down for the last time.

This humanism has a familiar feeling. It is reinforced every-where—in the media and in the very structure of our everyday lives. Even much of ministry practice, to some extent responding to the critiques of the psychological community, has for several generations been directed to this ethic of good works and common sense. The incorporation of secular psychological theory into clinical pastoral education became a melding of two congenial and related professions, both dedicated to mentally healthy individuals who can act in concert for the common social good. I firmly believe that this point of view undergirds most professional therapeutic and counseling encounters and is in fact the philosophical glue that has held our culture together for several centuries.

I would like to add a note here about why it may be difficult for secular humanists to hear "religious" messages from their clients. As noted, the humanist philosophical system fulfills a basic need for meaning within a modern scientific culture. And as a system, it has the same needs for boundary protection as any other system. In order not to dissolve into a dizzying blur, this system does what all the other systems do: it tends to hear whatever supports its presuppositions and to discount or ignore whatever does not. Though this is understandable and even desirable, it presents serious problems when, as frequently happens, religious clients encounter secular humanistic therapists because religious systems are based on an assumption that undermines a fundamental boundary premise of secular humanism—the premise that the supernatural is a projection of human needs, fears, and rationalizations. Furthermore, when the central reality question is one of cause and effect, we are engaged primarily in linear thinking and problem solving, and a suggestion of belief systems can seem off the track or irrelevant. The medical model itself—that there is a malfunction of some kind, a disequilibrium—lends itself to a search for the source of problems and, ideally, to the discovery of solutions. We are all so familiar with this model that I assume it needs no additional comment.

The essential life question humanism leads us to ask is, *What are the cause and effect?*

The Quest for Unity

Suppose we live as if our individual consciousness is merely an illusionary expression of a universal consciousness, in the same way that a wave is an expression of the ocean. And suppose we can learn to short-circuit the pain and confusion and selfishness of this world through simple techniques that will make this universal consciousness available to us. We assume that evil in the world stems from our separateness and from our selfish desires and that both goodness and happiness increase in direct proportion to our transcendence of individuality and our participation in higher awareness. In some sense the material world is an illusion and the existence that is real is that of the spirit.

There have been a number of popular formulations of this belief system (I think of Shirley MacLaine's books and other New

Age literature), and it is the basic stance of Buddhism and Hinduism. It is also an implicit stance of many Western mystics and is a "heresy" that the Christian church has continued to struggle with since early times. (The church respects its Jewish origin in insisting that God created and cherishes bodiliness and sees redemptive meaning in suffering.) The existential question that this stance infers, to me at least, is a goal that I will state (with apologies to those who practice these disciplines): *How can I supersede the selfish desires of my individual existence?*

This belief system sometimes seems to be religious, but I am including it here because it provides a stance in the universe that does not require a deity. Alan Watts ([1961] 1975) has even suggested that it is more of a psychology than a religion. Chanting, ascetic practices, psychedelic drugs, meditation, and other trance induction practices are illustrations of what I think of as modern therapeutic-religious practices deriving from this belief system. Describing them in these terms does not seem to do justice to the sophistication of ancient Eastern practices far beyond the limits of Western conceptualizations. However, this approach, coexisting with an increasing interest in alternative realities, is being treated with greater seriousness and respect in the West.

An interesting Christian mystical perspective that modifies and westernizes this stance is offered by the psychiatrist Gerald May in his book *Will and Spirit* (1982). He is interested in "unifying" experiences but does not perceive them as an escape from the pain of the world, and his model offers a conceptual bridge that might be useful for mental health professionals to consider. The psychologist Richard Mann has also discussed the implications of this perspective in *The Light of Consciousness* (1984).

Summary

Secular as ifs may have a metaphysical component, but they resemble one another in having no concept of God. In many ways they are "quasi-psychologies" in that they ask essentially psychological life questions: how can we be happy, what are the cause and effect of human experiences, and how can we supersede the selfish desires of our individual existence? In particular, the as if that we are labeling "humanism" undergirds most of Western civilization; it is so pervasive as to be nearly unnoticeable and is the philosophy underlying nearly all therapeutic systems.

Chapter Seven

Psychological As Ifs

Earlier we reviewed what I referred to as the anthropology of belief systems and suggested that in addition to core beliefs about the nature of existence that underlie our existential theories, core beliefs about the nature of the human being underlie our different psychological theories. Taking the broadest possible perspective, I would like now to suggest a number of anthropological premises that influence our choice of psychological as ifs. As with religious theories, I contend that these also are *choices*, not scientific absolutes.

Let us first review the development of modern psychology, which hints at the changes in underlying premises occurring over the past century. (I am indebted to my colleague Harold Edwards for this conceptualization.) Abraham Maslow (1969) pointed out that there have been four "forces" in the history of psychology, each one incorporating and building on the force that came earlier. He notes that, like most trends in science, psychology reflects the beliefs of its own culture. So when, during the first half of the twentieth century, religion was put on the sidelines by scientists who held that only phenomena that could be observed and measured were "real," psychology became a branch of the biological sciences. The human being was explained as the highest form of animal life, nothing more, and mental activity was believed to be a product of biological processes only. This psychology was called "behaviorism." However, behaviorism required severe disregard for a whole spectrum of human experiences, so when Sigmund Freud began to talk about the "unconscious mind," it was a relief once again to pay attention to our rich inner lives. Freud's system, psychoanalysis, eventually became the predominant force in the science of psychology—a "second force," if you will.

The theories of both behaviorism and psychoanalysis grew primarily out of work with mentally ill people, which peculiarly skewed their conclusions about human functioning. Around 1950 it occurred to a number of psychologists that in order to understand the human personality, it would make sense to study emotionally healthy people rather than sick ones. Out of these early studies of happy and successful individuals came a new psychology known as "humanistic psychology." But the insights of the earlier psychologies of behaviorism and psychoanalysis continued to be important. As individuals explored their passions and fears, they realized that they were indeed greatly influenced by repressed memories and emotions, as Freud had taught. Also, as successful organizations such as Alcoholics Anonymous focused on corrective behavior, many of the early assertions of the behaviorists proved to be powerful factors in changing destructive habits.

However, something was missing. The human being was still viewed as merely a highly evolved animal. Yet paranormal events such as clairvoyance, telepathy, and precognition continued to occur in many people's lives and did not fit the explanations of the early humanistic psychologists. At first the explorations of these events, conducted by psychologists at Duke University and elsewhere, were scoffed at, but as ideas from the Eastern religions and scholarly explorations of altered states of consciousness became subjects of popular interest, psychologists began to wonder, among other things, how individuals could make intuitive leaps in perception and understanding without, seemingly, any basis in knowledge or experience. Eventually a new school, "transpersonal psychology," began to emerge. It focused on what is outside the bounds of scientific knowledge and on the intuitive.

As we noted in Chapter One, early in the twentieth century, the psychologist William James had studied the religious function in human life. It was not until seventy years later, when Freud's estranged colleague Carl Jung (who was always fascinated by the role of the transcendent) was rediscovered, that life's mysteries began to be taken seriously within the psychological community. Jung's insights have resulted in a system that anticipates transpersonal psychology and has been increasingly influential in recent decades.

In each of the psychologies described, as-if assumptions about the nature of the human being underlie the therapeutic system. As we did with secular as ifs in Chapter Six, I would like to examine these psychological systems and show how unarticulated premises govern the conclusions each has reached. In addition, I will briefly allude to several other psychological systems that emphasize still different aspects of the human being: systems theory and what have been called "body therapies."

Behaviorism

Suppose we proceed as if human beings are primarily animals adapting to their environment through natural selection, as all animals do. Thoughts and feelings are merely adaptive mechanisms facilitating the process. The success of human life, both individually and collectively, is determined by various kinds of reinforcements, both positive and negative, and can be influenced through the manipulation of these reinforcements. We are concerned with cause and effect, and especially with behaviors, not feeling states, because for reinforcements to be scientifically applied, behavior changes must be measurable. We assume that all of life is conditioned by past experience and that there is no such thing as "free will." Behaviorists seek "objective" evidence and have no interest in emotions, wishes, and talents, which are a priori factors, called "contingencies," a sort of wastebasket term for anything that cannot be measured. The founder of modern behaviorism, B. F. Skinner (1953), believed that if it were possible to control contingencies, all of human life could be explained in behavioral terms.

Behavior therapy has proved especially effective in institutional settings like schools, prisons, and treatment centers where contingencies can be controlled. It is also the commonsense method used over the centuries by parents everywhere: if you eat your peas, you may have dessert; after you clean your room, you may go out to play.

Psychoanalysis

Suppose we proceed as if Freud was right. We will stress that humans are set apart from the other animals by their ability to reason, imagine, and, especially, remember. Our focus will be on unconscious memories that influence our behavior, feelings, and motivation. We accept two dominant controls over human behavior: repressed thoughts and emotions, and instinctual drives, especially sexual and aggressive drives. We believe that if repressed thoughts and emotions could be made conscious, humans could live relatively unobstructed and productive lives. We assert that the overt human personality is merely a psychic "skin" enclosing an unconscious emotional caldron of unseen and unknown power and energy outside of ordinary awareness. This interior inferno has the capacity to erupt into psychosis and aggression or into a multitude of creative or destructive thoughts and feelings.

If we subscribe to this understanding of the human personality, psychoanalytic theory will be our point of departure in the understanding of the human being. We will be concerned with the structure of the unconscious and with how it organizes our psychic energy, with the id and the ego and the superego, with libido and cathexis, with transference and countertransference—so many of the terms in our contemporary psychological vocabulary come out of this tradition.

Modern civilization without Freud's insights can hardly be imagined. We would live in a peculiar sort of psychological flat-earth world without the concept of the unconscious mind. Psychoanalytic theory postulates a complex set of ideas about how the human personality is constructed and differs from behavioral theory principally in its focus on internal unconscious processes. Psychoanalytic theory has provided the seed bed for most of the humanistic psychologies, including transactional analysis, Gestalt therapy, neurolinguistic programming, and analytical psychology.

Freud's assumption that God is merely a construct of the human imagination caused a major split between religion and psychology, even though this point of view predates Freud by several hundred years and was the cultural norm for educated persons of his own day. From the point of view of a religious client, this existential blind spot is tragic because the elegance and beauty of the best of psychoanalytic theory has been anathema for so many religious people.

Humanistic Psychology

Suppose we proceed as if human beings have an inner healing capacity that can promote health and "wholeness." Psychologists such as Maslow and Carl Rogers discovered that if individuals were helped to tune in to their own inner resources, they had within themselves a powerful impulse toward emotional health. On the basis of his studies of motivation and personality, Maslow (1962) advanced the idea that human beings have unrealized potentials that can be "actualized." He explored the ways in which successful and accomplished people had, in fact, actualized their gifts. He raised the question of what kinds of experiences facilitate human growth, and various experiments in new behaviors and interactions gave birth to what came to be known as the human potential movement. Freedom to explore existential boundaries and to overcome arrested or distorted physical, mental, and emotional development became the goal.

Techniques have been steadily developed outside the traditional psychological community for realizing the "more" that is possible in human life. For one thing, it was discovered that when people got together in groups, something about the group process itself helped members grow emotionally. (Therapy and growth groups are so common these days that it is hard to remember that only a few years ago they were highly suspect within the psychological community.) Humanistic psychology took a big step in bringing psychology into the lives of ordinary people. There was no longer a need to identify oneself as crazy to use the resources of psychology.

Transpersonal Psychology

Going one step further, suppose we proceed as if human beings can experience mysterious forces outside of the understanding of conventional science. Suppose that ESP, precognition, and other paranormal events provide clues to energy fields and varieties of consciousness of which we have as yet only hints. We sense that we are more than merely physical beings, the highest order of animals, but are in fact spiritual beings with enigmatic intuitive abilities not explainable by conventional science.

As we noted, this newest school of psychology incorporates the perspectives of the other three—behaviorism, psychoanalysis, and humanistic psychology—but insists that a mysterious additional capability has to be taken into account, especially in explaining the psychology of creativity. It opens the possibility of studying paranormal events formerly relegated to the realm of superstition and coincidence and challenges us to understand the mysteries of creativity in more depth.

Analytical Psychology

Suppose we believe that there is a "collective unconscious"— that the conscious individual personality is afloat in a sea of unconscious forces of which it is a singular manifestation. The individual can dip into this collective unconscious through meditation, dreams, guided images, artistic endeavors, and the like. The collective unconscious may be equated in some way with God, but this is not necessary. Jung called his therapeutic system "analytical psychology," and interest in its application is increasing within the psychological and religious communities because it seems to integrate the understandings of both. As previously observed, various meditation approaches have also been popular as ways to experience some sort of collective unconscious through the temporary abrogating of individual awareness in order to allow dreamlike images and archetypes to emerge.

Analytical psychology, in its traditional form, is particularly concerned with dream analysis and with the influence of predetermined personality types. Dreams and fantasies outside the arena of normal awareness are considered helpful in deepening subconscious contact with the higher Self, and Jung was especially fascinated with the way universal archetypes express themselves in individual lives and how we subvert our higher selves.

Jungian psychology has insinuated itself into many popular therapies. For example, guided imagery has introduced thousands of Americans to a helpful way to meditate, and hypnosis has reemerged as a serious therapeutic technique. Religious Jungian psychologists are experimenting with dream interpretations using religious symbols, and spiritual guidance centers are incorporating Jungian theory into their work.

Systems Theory

Suppose we notice that the individual is merely a unit in a concentric circle of ever larger systems—the family, the neighborhood, the community, and so on—and a change in any part of any of these systems inevitably changes the system itself. It is futile even to consider individuals as separate units. Therefore, a study of the laws and forces governing systems is imperative, and mental health interventions will occur at the level of whatever size system seems to be most affected by disequilibrium. This body of systems theory is currently enjoying great popularity in the larger community of sciences, both physical and social, and is directly responsible for the underlying premises of this book.

Body Therapies

But that is not all. Suppose we live as if our bodies are ourselves. We decide to attend to the "instrument" of our individualities, the human body itself. Suppose we note that we only think and act and feel what our bodies allow us. We hold our past miseries and traumas rigidly in what Wilhelm Reich referred to as "body armor," and because of this we are tremendously limited by our physical incarnations. Our bodies depress us and excite us and transport us. When we free our bodies to be fully alive, our thoughts and feelings are correspondingly freed. But our bodies are not merely protoplasmic machines. They are, above all, energy fields, and so the therapeutic tasks are to attend to both the protoplasm (muscles, skeleton, organs, and so on) and the flow of energy. The great popularity of yoga in recent years attests to interest in this aspect of our humanness, and the psychologies of bioenergetics, Gestalt, polarity, and rebirthing, among others, are only beginning to explore all the possibilities of working with the body.

Summary

Mental health theory operates from several aggressively differing belief systems. None of us—neither religious people nor mental health professionals—comprehends the whole truth, no matter how frequently we may behave as though we do. Just as we can never know the final nature of reality, captured inside of space-time-energy-matter as we are, so also we can never explain the complex and ephemeral human being entirely from one theoretical model.

Mental health professionals encounter belief systems in their professional theories, in their personal lives, and in the lives of their clients. As we have observed, whenever an unmanageable field of data, feelings, and experiences is organized into a "paradigm"—a model that creates order out of chaos—a belief system exists. However, as we have attempted to illustrate, the same chaotic field of human experience can be organized in many ways. A personal choice, whether religious or psychological, is not scientific—despite mountains of "proof" in both psychology and theology intended to demonstrate the absolute validity of particular beliefs—but rather, as we have discussed earlier, is a matter of opinion. And as William James argued, having opinions about reality is not optional; we all have them.

This brief presentation of psychoanalytic theory, behaviorism, humanistic psychology, transpersonal psychology, analytical psychology, systems theory, and the body therapies is simply illustrative of various psychological foci that become increasingly complex as the human personality is better understood. But it is important to note that *all* of them seem true and probably none of them is wholly true.

Chapter Eight

—

Religious As Ifs

We come now to as ifs that involve belief in God. Most people in the world, and more than half in this country, live as if God were a reality. So no matter how uncomfortable that assumption makes professionals in the mental health world, there is no possible way to study belief systems without devoting a major chapter to religious ideas. However, as I stated earlier, religious affiliation does not necessarily tell us anything about a person's core beliefs, and conversely, understanding the as ifs that govern an individual's life does not necessarily tell us what religious system that person fits them into. So while I will be making allusions to Western religious systems in this chapter, these will be for the sake of illustration only and not because there are no other religious systems equally appropriate to the beliefs under study.

Personal Salvation

Suppose we live as if God is a personal friend. Suppose in fact we assume, as the Mormons do, that God is really a person. Or suppose we accept the classic Christian doctrine that God is three persons in one. Suppose we take literally Jesus' description of God as a Loving Father. Or suppose we subscribe to one of the divergent sects that preach this message through a particular guru. We are God's actual children, and God cares for each of us personally—communicates with us, listens to us, and intervenes directly, regularly, and effectively in our everyday lives. God cares what happens to us. We are not alone in a cold and impersonal universe, mere accidents of fate, but rather are made in the mysterious image of a deeply loving and personal creator. We do not edit away allusions in the Bible to God's granting our hearts' desires. If bad things happen to us, they happen for reasons that we can eventually understand. We believe that all things work together for good for those who love God, even if we cannot see the emerging patterns as they occur. We believe that because God loves us as individuals, He will preserve our individuality in the world to come. In other words, we believe that God is dedicated to personal and individual salvation in the most literal sense. We will meet again in the next life, and we will know each other as persons.

I think this life stance is especially difficult for most mental health people. There is a projective quality about it, a quality of wishful thinking; God is every child's perfect parent. It has been my experience that therapists frequently desire to help their clients understand the neurotic basis for these beliefs by exploring such issues as how their parents might have failed them or, conversely, overindulged them or how they can meet their leftover childish needs in more constructive and realistic ways. I do not mean to suggest that this intervention is overt; I suspect it is usually buried in other questions and suggestions so as to be inferred rather than stated directly. But I strongly believe that clients often know this and therefore fail to share their deep sense of God's personal presence in their lives or believe (sometimes correctly) that therapy will not be possible because professionals will discount their faith.

It is of course true that this stance also shows up in the thought content of many overtly psychotic individuals. I will take up the question of discernment of psychosis in Chapter Fourteen. Although this is not the place for a theological justification of faith in personal salvation, I would observe that it is held by many mature adults who do not seem to need substitute parents. Excellent apologetics are available. Nor is this the place to detail the many well-documented instances of what have seemed to be personal interventions in individual lives by a mysterious force that is frequently and confidently asserted to be God; William James ([1902] 1958) fills his book with them. This discussion is merely an attempt to ask you to suspend disbelief long enough to imagine what the world would be like if a certain life view is assumed to be true.

To heighten the impact of this, imagine that tonight you are wakened by the sense of a blinding light and that you experience a quality of bliss that seems inexplicable. In the morning the sense of well-being continues, and a conviction begins to grow almost outside of awareness that something mysterious and benevolent and wonderful has happened, and this awareness continues over time. Would you seek help for your new "neurosis"? Would you tell anyone? Are you sure of that? (Most people who have such inexplicable experiences do not, in fact, tell anyone.) Would it change your life? How? Would you become less fearful, less cynical, even less cautious?

I have described what I am convinced is a fairly common "conversion" experience. Though research subjects do not necessarily identify these peak experiences as religious, the theologian Urban Holmes III (1980) notes that people tend to use available cultural norms as explanations and that where religion is normative, they will use familiar religious metaphors—which is, of course, the point of this discussion.

As I will detail later, there is a great need for good therapy for these converted persons, not because the conversion makes them crazy, but because a conversion experience may free them for profound self-examination in other areas of their lives. God and therapy can frequently walk hand in hand. Conversion should be a marvelous tool in the therapeutic process because it can, among other consequences, lead to further personal growth and self-awareness. It allows both the religious question *How and where do I encounter God?* and the therapeutic question *What is expected of me?*

Cocreationism

Suppose we live as if we are cocreators with God of the kingdom of heaven. This hypothesis is assuming increasing importance in Christian theological circles, especially in Roman Catholic circles, and I need to indulge in a little Christian theology in order to explain it. In some ways it is a religious expression of the secular radicalism of the 1960s. In Christian terminology, the kingdom of God or the kingdom of heaven or, as Martin Luther King, Jr., referred to it, the beloved community is that ideal community in which God's plan for us is somehow realized. Christian tradition has tended to project it into the future and to call it heaven. However, Jesus sometimes referred to it as present among us now or even inside each of us. This seemingly esoteric philosophy is much more popular than might be supposed. Matthew Fox (1984) has written several widely read books based on the idea that God did not condemn us, as the believers in original sin contend, but rather blessed us to enrich and care for the earth and each other.

This stance accepts the evidence of evolution that history has a goal and a purpose, even if it is such a simple one as the perpetuation of the species, and it suggests that everything in the world continuously changes in response to this evolutionary impulse. With the emergence of self-awareness in *Homo sapiens*, evolution came under the control of consciousness rather than chance and natural selection. And with the emergence of moral awareness, evolution increasingly became a moral enterprise.

This perspective seems to provide a much more social goal than the others with which we have dealt. Though I have presented the Christian perspective, I gather that a significant number of Muslims have similar aspirations, and of course the core impulse behind Zionism is the re-creation of God's holy land (kingdom) of Israel. The therapeutic question is not only personal but also socioeconomic: *How do we change?* If we are each responsible for the coming of the kingdom, then from the Christian perspective we must act together to banish hatred, war, and injustice. Together we must become messengers of peace and love. We are God's instruments in this world. Furthermore, we must strive together to clarify our understanding of what the kingdom is to be like. We must become communities because our neighbors are ourselves. We must be enablers, no longer only ministers and therapists. We must be visionaries and truth tellers. The biggest of all possible religious questions is addressed by this perspective: *Who shall we become?*

To repeat, I do not mean to imply that Christians have a corner on this question. We alluded earlier to the Enlightenment, when secular idealists suggested alternatives to the divine right of kings. In those times, Western religion had been co-opted by government, and reform was inevitably secular. In our own time, Marxism has seriously addressed the question, and in Latin America, the liberation theologians struggle with a Christian Marxism. Zionists address the question from the Jewish perspective, and the various segments of Islam find passionate answers to the question in the areas of the world where they have control. But everywhere, *Who shall we become?* is seen as a religious question.

Even within the therapeutic world, the direction is toward the creation of community. Systems theory, therapeutic communities, group therapy, milieu therapy, family therapy, and voluntary groups all point away from a focus solely on the individual. Some utopian schemes, therapeutic versions of the kingdom, fail; the pioneers of deinstitutionalization look back sadly on their visions. But the impulse is very similar to the kingdom visions that propel religious people, the sense that there must be a better way, an image of a loving community. Our visions are not so different; we simply give them different names.

Evangelical Christianity

Finally, suppose we live as if no one gets to heaven except through Jesus. This is the basic Christian evangelical belief that a single person, the human-divine person known as Jesus Christ, is the sole and exclusive path to a literal in-the-future, end-time heaven and that his message is literally "given" in the Bible. For fundamentalist Christians, this means faith, not in the historical Jesus Christ, but in the still-alive person manifested in spirit form, known as the Holy Spirit. One opens oneself to the Holy Spirit, and Jesus becomes present through a conversion experience referred to as "rebirth." One's life is then changed completely, and one turns it over to Jesus, who then uses it for the realization of divine purposes in the world.

Religious fundamentalism has become the whipping boy of both psychology and the liberal religions. The same kind of polarization seems to exist in the religious world that exists in politics. "That Roosevelt is going to ruin this country," my conservative relatives confidently asserted during the 1930s. "That Oral Roberts nonsense is going to blow up the world," assert mainline Christians and Jews in the 1990s. It will be a premise of this discussion that it should be possible to think about religion the way we think about politics. There is a left wing and a right wing, and they both have a piece of the truth. We need not even say that the middle way is true. Religion and politics may also be like elephants, and having hold of the trunk or the tail of either does not mean that one grasps the whole beast. Indeed, I personally doubt that it is possible to grasp the whole beast; we have to do our best with the parts we have our hands on. It does no good to shout at the fellow with the long, fat, snorting part with the hole in it that he does not really perceive correctly. He deals as best he can with what he has, and he is well advised to stand back when it takes a snootful of water, even though we at the other end have to be wary of a different sort of consequence.

Is there a therapeutic question that Christian fundamentalists might ask? I think they would turn to Scripture and ask what guidance can be derived from God's word. So the religious and therapeutic questions are the same: *What is Jesus' message for me, and what is its meaning in my life?*

Summary

I have tried in the last three chapters to suggest ways in which some common belief systems are created: how different assumptions about reality ("as ifs") raise inevitable life questions in the secular, psychological, and religious worlds. In all cases, the beliefs we have described organize existential chaos and reduce existential anxiety—those two purposes we identified as underlying belief systems of whatever origin. In the next chapter, we will take each of these life questions and attempt to suggest therapeutic approaches that might be appropriate.

Chapter Nine

~

Implications for Practice

When my mother died, she was eighty-eight years old, blind and deaf, confused, and bitterly unhappy. About three weeks before she died, she suddenly stopped chewing her food, resisted sitting in a chair, and became incontinent. Without either our request or our knowledge, a resident psychiatrist from the community mental health center came to see her in the nursing home where she lived and recommended to us that she be admitted to the university hospital and given shock treatments "for her depression." I was horrified. Though it was true that she had been depressed for many years and had responded favorably to Prozac, it seemed to me that something different was going on this time. The nursing staff was sure that she was getting ready to die and felt that we should no longer push her into physical activity, so to my great relief it was decided that we would ignore the mental health recommendation. We all felt that psychiatric "correctness" had replaced both compassion and common sense.

After she died, I got a phone call from the supervising psychiatric gerontologist—he had been seeing my mother in his office about once a month—saying that he was sorry her case "had not had a happier outcome." I replied that I thought her case had had a *very* happy outcome—she died. And feeling irritated by the insensitive intrusion of his subordinate from the mental health center, I later wrote him a letter in which, among other things, I wondered if the gerontology staff had an articulated philosophy about death, as it seemed to me that my mother's depression was serving a useful purpose. "Suppose," I ventured, "her depression had lifted enough for her to be terrified by what was happening to her. Would that have been a good thing?"

Looking back on the whole episode, I think now that everyone involved was attempting to do "case planning" at the intersection of at least three divergent belief systems and that some of our misunderstandings arose from those differences—first and foremost my mother's: Mother thought she was going to go to hell after she died; she told us so specifically. It was not an illogical conclusion, given the level of her senile paranoia; no wonder she was depressed. My admittedly subjective assessment is that somewhere along the line she had tried to impose evangelical television Christianity onto an amalgam of liberal humanism and scientific skepticism and thus had no integrated core belief with which to confront her guilt and self-hatred. Assurances from all of us who were caring for her had no impact at all. But I am absolutely sure that an easy death for my mother could only have come from as much confusion and numbness as her psychological defenses could muster, and I am thankful that we did not interfere. (As far as we know, she slipped away peacefully in the night.)

My own core belief is that death is part of life and that whatever happens to us after we die is a continuation of what happened in this life. I hope that death is not the absolute end, whether bitter or otherwise, and I also hope that my mother will have her wish granted to be reincarnated as one of my sister's cats so she can receive the tender care and lavish affection denied her in the life from which she just departed; I am being only partly whimsical in wishing this because I believe that a universe that contains giraffes and tropical fish could just as well as not contain souls reincarnated as animals.

I have no way of knowing what the psychiatrists believed in— "science," I presume, and depression as a bad thing. I appreciated what I assume was their primary belief that it is never too late to try to improve a person's mental health, to aim for self-understanding and self-acceptance. I have no idea how they felt about death. Fear? Avoidance? Is death a friend or an enemy? My sense is that they would reply, "Neither. Death happens." But as far as I know, death was not part of the doctor's discussions with my mother, and certainly it never came up with me.

What did the nurses believe? They seemed comfortable with the ebbing lives all around them. They were the people we could talk with about death, the ones who comforted and reassured us, who believed in cushioning the transition from this life with as much freedom from pain and fear as possible. Did they believe that anything came next? I do not know. But they understood that my mother's death affected us all; each of us may die alone, but the void created by that solitary surrender rearranges the psyches and interconnectedness of all whose lives border the now-empty space and reminds us that we may be next.

A nursing home is the best place I can think of to confront ultimate questions. It is a crucible of physical and mental illness, family strength and pathology, religious convictions and practices, and institutional structures, services, strengths, and weaknesses. It may be possible to be psychologically dispassionate and theoretical with young adults (in good health), but throw in precarious health, physical handicap, or old age, and suddenly our passions are engaged. (We check ourselves in the mirror at night—is that mole getting larger? Is that a dimple in my breast? Why is my color so bad? I reassure myself that I don't have to think about that; so far, so good.) As a professional, I find reasons not to visit my clients in nursing homes—too time-consuming, too distracting. Or more commonly, I remind myself that young people offer the best prospects for psychotherapy—they are more malleable, less set in their ways, more intellectually alert.

Talk of core beliefs and mental health theory is easy in the abstract. But my mother's situation reminds us, not only that it would have been helpful had all concerned been aware of differences in belief systems, but also that those beliefs were affecting the ways in which we approached her impending death. It also reminds us that it is one thing to identify the variety of belief systems that individuals use to cope with the chaos of life and quite another to go beyond mere identification and attempt to incorporate such understanding into everyday mental health counseling or therapy. I am astonished by the frequency with which mental health professionals duck the opportunity to explore beliefs by suggesting that clients "talk to their ministers" at times of existential crisis or when alternative realities happen to surface, as if most ministers are more ready to deal with the spiritual, the irrational, and the mystical than therapists are. As we have discussed, in their effort to incorporate religion into the mainstream, to make it "relevant," many churches have lost their other-worldliness altogether, and what spiritual seekers may discover when they take their concerns to their ministers is sometimes nothing more than watered-down psychotherapy. (Fortunately, this is not always true; many ministers and priests remain helpful allies in spiritual quests.)

Knowing all this, how do we open our own counseling practices to spiritual concerns? How do we cross that fragile line from our own belief system to our clients', exploring theirs yet preserving our own? How could the psychiatrists involved with my mother have honored her bleak and paranoid outlook, which was not going to change at that point in her life, without thrusting her into intolerable alertness and terror? How could they have honored the nurses' and family's conviction that in her situation, death would be a blessing?

Mental health practice has many dimensions, as my mother's situation illustrates. More and more we are realizing that intervention needs to occur in nontraditional settings such as nursing homes and that it needs to have many dimensions, ranging from one-session crisis intervention to years-long psychoanalysis. On a "depth" scale, professionals find themselves ranging from simple problem solving to effecting profound personality change, so that assessment and intervention strategies vary according to the needs and goals of the client or clients. (It may have occurred to you that the psychiatric people involved with my mother could have had three sets of clients, not just one: the patient, her family, and her caregivers.)

Fundamentals of Practice

Let us now consider how belief systems can become part of a counseling practice. To do this we need to think briefly about some fundamentals. No matter what the discipline, whether psychiatry or social work or pastoral counseling (to mention only a few), every case goes through seven basic stages: contact, relationship building, assessment, goal setting, intervention, evaluation, and termination. Though some of these may happen simultaneously—it is frequently impossible to separate assessment and intervention, for example, and relationship building is ongoing—I have always alleged that all seven must eventually occur, and there are some techniques for incorporating attention to beliefs into these. I also want to observe that the contact and relationship phases are very different for the different professions, such that pastors, school counselors, and psychiatric nurses, for example, may already have relationships with clients and know at least part of their histories in ways that psychiatrists or social workers do not.

Contact and Relationship

Even in the contact phase, a concern on the part of the client about who the therapist or counselor is—that person's background and basic philosophy—should be addressed. It will often be the first time the client's very legitimate interest in whether or not the therapist can appreciate his or her point of view will surface. The person making the initial contact can ask, "Do you have anyone in particular you would like to talk with?" My Muslim client's desire to talk with someone who believed in God was an unusually direct example of this, but sometimes clients will suggest their worries about the identity of the therapist in more indirect ways by indicating a need to be seen in a particular setting or to have an older counselor or specifically a man or a woman. Pursuing the reasons for these requests ("You wanted to see a woman?") can uncover issues that might not otherwise come up.

Relationships between clients and therapists are dependent on professional communication and listening skills, and these affect the inclusion of beliefs into the content of the interview. The Gestalt therapist Erv Polster refers to therapy as a "dance" in which there is lively back-and-forth-ness between therapist and client, and everything is "grist for the mill" (see Polster and Polster, 1973). In this model of therapy, the therapist is not a blank screen onto which the client's thoughts and feelings are projected but rather an active instrument in an ongoing exchange, using reactions to the client's thoughts and feelings as a "resonating chamber" with which to heighten the shared experience. This means, of course, that the therapist or counselor's ideas, reactions, and beliefs are a vital part of the interaction; the counselor is, in therapeutic terminology, "transparent," as I was willing to be transparent when I shared my belief in God with my Muslim client in Chapter One.

As we all know, there are dangers in therapist transparency: the danger that the therapist will unduly influence the client, that the therapist's own pathology will be superimposed on the client's, or that irreconcilable differences will surface that could be avoided if the therapist were to keep silent. But in my judgment these dangers are mitigated by two factors that are always present with nonpsychotic clients. The first is that clients tend to hear what they want to hear; within reason, it is not necessary to walk on eggs when on the therapist's side of the table. The other is that more often than not, the worst thing that can happen in a therapeutic exchange is that *nothing* will happen.

The advantages of therapist transparency are several. First, it is my experience that it greatly increases trust because the client can then assess the risks of sharing frightening or embarrassing fears and fantasies. And second, it allows the counselor's own strengths to be shared with the client, reducing the client's sense of isolation and strangeness. Because beliefs about reality constitute the absolute ground on which any of us stands, it is truly a scary act of faith to offer personal beliefs to another person for examination and approval.

Communication of religious beliefs is like communication of any other private area of an individual's life—the counselor must give tacit permission for it to be included in the conversation. In ordinary social exchanges, we do not bring up such precious personal subjects as our religious beliefs, just as we do not bring up the intimate subject of sex. Yet most counselors have been taught how to give permission for sex to be discussed. The word is used in a direct question or suggestion ("Tell me about your sex life"), or, if the client brings it up, the counselor responds with encouragement and nonjudgmental support. Exactly the same technique is helpful when exploration of beliefs seems appropriate.

I want to stress the importance of follow-up if a client tentatively mentions religion or the word *God,* no matter how casually. Trial balloons are floated by clients as well as by therapists. And listening for religious content is sometimes tricky; as we have discussed earlier, church membership is not necessarily a reliable guide to existential belief. Often there are conversational clues: "You may think this is crazy" is one, or "I suppose this is silly," both of which indicate embarrassment at broaching a subject that is somewhat out of the ordinary. Sometimes a story about a seemingly paranormal event will provide a lead-in, or a story about the beliefs of some close friend or relative. It is surprising that if one is listening for a particular subject, it will tend to appear, or, conversely, if a subject makes the counselor uncomfortable, it will never seem to be relevant to whatever is going on.

On the surface it may seem that this implies that we can only counsel persons with whom we share a belief system, but I am convinced there are broad parameters within which understanding of beliefs that differ from our own is possible. For example, both my Muslim client and I realized that our concepts of God were different; we elected not to go into those differences, and I was careful to explore her concepts at every stage of our relationship and not to impose mine. In my mother's situation, I assume that none of us shared her bleak outlook about the future, but had the psychiatrists known about it, they could at least have facilitated her confusion and denial, or if we had told them about her fantasy to be a pampered cat, they could perhaps have reinforced that image.

Assessment and Goal Setting

During the relationship building we have just discussed, assessment is continuously happening. But another specific method for assessment, which has fallen on hard times in recent years, also needs to be considered. I want to advocate here for the old-fashioned taking of case histories. We have become so problem-focused in our practices and so concerned not to become awash in irrelevancies that often client histories are either ignored or allowed to reveal themselves only during the course of interviews on other subjects. Clients are encouraged to set the agenda. But it has been my experience that even a relatively brief life history is a gold mine of revelatory information, both for the therapist *and for the client*, and this is especially true in long-term cases where life direction and meaning should be part of the overall goal because, as the psychiatrist Arthur Rifkin (1986) has observed, traditional therapy can tell us about the past, but it has nothing essential to say about the future, and the future, we should never forget, is where we are all going.

I have found that temporarily setting aside the presenting problem and deliberately taking therapy time for telling the story of the client's life (and I often put it just that way—"Tell me the story of your life") opens up possibilities in surprisingly helpful ways. In fact, when this is done by married couples in each other's presence, a whole new dimension of understanding often emerges. As Erv Polster (1987) has noted, seeing one's life as a story helps give all its events, good and bad, some meaning and, I would add, often reveals the individual's core beliefs.

Goal setting and interventions can also be expanded when more than simple problem identification and solution are relevant to the client's situation. Using Rifkin's image again, I like to think about turning the client's face toward the future. As noted earlier, there are helpful interventions that address the future rather than merely the past (unsnarling the past is, I presume, something we are all trained to do)—we help our clients discover particular ways in which their beliefs reduce angst and organize the chaos in their lives and thus enable them to feel relatively peaceful about what lies ahead.

Intervention Strategies

Two intervention strategies directly reinforce belief systems. We noted earlier that both religious and psychological belief systems are concerned with *love* (object relationships and, as we will describe in a moment, prayer relationships) and with *metaphors* (dreams, fantasies, myths, dogmas, and the arts). So the first strategy has to do with relationships—identifying them, strengthening them, and finding new ones—and the second has to do with discovering the metaphors that have meaning in the individual's life.

Love is, I suppose, the ultimate source of consolation and a sense of safety—of a reduction of angst, to use our earlier terminology. Everyone has had the experience of feeling safer in a threatening situation if a loved companion was there, no matter how irrational the feeling may be. (I once asked my husband to accompany me to the bathhouse at a campground full of bears. "What exactly," he asked me, "do you think I am going to do about a bear if we run into one?") But in addition to "object relations" with people, relationships can also be purely subjective. Very religious clients may tell you that they have a "relationship with God" if they are asked the question explicitly. (I doubt that anyone would say it to a secular counselor unless asked.) I am suggesting that the statement may mean exactly what it says, but unless you are prepared to take prayer life seriously, you are unlikely to discover all that the statement implies. Certainly, also, many clients have significant relationships with their churches, if by "relationship" we mean feelings of love and responsibility. (If it seems odd to think of a relationship with an institution, think about how you feel about your family as an institutional system.) Furthermore, artists frequently feel love for and responsibility to their artistic muse; I have found that they often take intense interest in exploring the nature of this relationship with their particular art ("How do you feel when you are painting? What does it mean to you?") and report a sense of unity and centeredness during their creative times.

Of course, artistic expression and appreciation are also metaphorical, and that invokes the second intervention strategy we are considering. But even though we are accustomed to exploring the metaphors in clients' dreams and fantasies, we are less comfortable with their belief metaphors, particularly if these are religious. By asking the client to show the therapist a particularly cherished icon, religious picture, or other possession or to share a poem or story, the religious metaphors that organize the chaos in the client's life can begin to become apparent and core beliefs can start to surface.

But a word of warning is warranted here. Before a client will feel comfortable sharing religious thoughts, feelings, and artifacts, the client needs assurance that the therapist accepts these as real. "Real" in this context means having some absolute importance outside of the individual's subjective experience. In light of the nearly universal suspicion of therapy, therapists must know how they would answer a question such as "Do you think I'm just making this up?" or "Do you think all this is just in my head?" This is why I made such a point of objective versus subjective experience earlier; I find it helpful to remind myself that we each organize reality out of the combination of our subjective and objective experience, and to the extent that I can say to my client, "I don't know what 'real' means, but I find everyone's ideas interesting and helpful," I give permission to share that personal vision of reality.

Erv Polster suggests casting the individual's entire life in metaphorical terms to create an individual "novel," another way of excavating belief systems. "What is your life telling you?" becomes a relevant question. For religious clients, again, subjective identification with a religious or biblical person can be revealing. Even single words can be metaphorical; my therapist used the term *wellspring* as a metaphor for my religious life, and that image has had complex and continuing importance to me. (I have wondered if exploring the image of a reincarnated cat would have comforted my mother.) As organizers of chaos, metaphors are supremely effective and can be introduced into a client's life as a specific intervention. And finding ongoing metaphors, whether religious practices, aesthetic experiences, or creative endeavors, can help clients bring order and meaning into the unknown future.

Evaluation and Termination

The termination phase of any therapeutic relationship has special significance. As a personal preference, I am of the open-door school of therapy—I never view therapy as terminated. But episodes of mental health interventions do come to an end, and I hope that some day I will hear about imaginative, bold therapeutic relationships that include some sort of ritual at the time of termination. It seems to me that already common group rituals such as writing a story together or creating a painting or rituals of giving thanks to each participant could be extended to individual therapy as well. I hope all readers who are members of the clergy already begin and end sessions with a ritual observance such as a prayer or a moment of silence, but to the extent that beliefs become important in a more secular setting, the exchange of tokens can signal the affirmation of those beliefs: the therapist's signature in a book, for instance, or a photograph of the client's most significant place or object. Termination should do for therapy what the blessing at the end of a religious ceremony does: put the seal of approval and hope on what has gone before.

Practice in Nontraditional Settings

Most mental health interventions occur in places other than counselors' offices. School counselors and nurses, family doctors, group leaders, group home workers, prison wardens and guards, police and other law enforcement officials—all are confronted daily with mental health problems and respond effectively or not, depending on the level of their professional training and their personal sensitivity. One educator, discussing intervention with children in school, pointed out that we take advantage of "windows of opportunity." The moment of disequilibrium, of crisis even, is the moment when an individual is open to change, and the benefit of being "in the field" with clients is that those windows of opportunity can immediately be taken advantage of.

A vivid illustration of such an opportunity, and of the contribution that professionals can make, comes out of my own experience as a TB patient and has to do with the genesis of my own belief system. It began with my first awareness of death—I was, I suppose, six or seven years old. My rationally secular parents assured me that it was sort of like "going to sleep forever" but that I wouldn't have to worry about it for many years to come. However, by the time I was in my teens, I had figured out that death could in fact occur to anyone at any time (World War II had just begun), and a certain panic about the idea of going to sleep forever had set in. So when I became hospitalized, the panic achieved an immediacy that kept me awake nights.

To my everlasting gratitude, a compassionate doctor took a chance by offering me an irregular intervention. Suspecting that I was desperate in my misery, the doctor, after some preliminary questions about how I was feeling, hesitantly asked if I had any religious beliefs. I remember that she then told me about her own religious conversion following the death of a close friend, and somehow that brave sharing took some of the embarrassment out of the whole encounter. Her question startled me a little because I had been secretly listening with fascination to a radio evangelist (this was before TV) and had previously gone to an Episcopal church with friends on Christmas Eve and Easter, though I had no formal religious connections. The doctor picked up on the allusion to the Episcopal church and asked if I would like the minister from that church to come to see me. I must have agreed because shortly thereafter the Reverend Henry Lewis appeared at my bedside carrying an armload of books—another particularly effective response. He had learned that I was a reader and had guessed that the best response to my religious needs might be a literary one.

From the perspective of this discussion, these were both excellent mental health interventions. Neither the minister nor the doctor was identified as a mental health professional, but their responses to my emotional need zeroed in on its central component, my craving for some sort of belief system that would relieve my fear of death and provide a way to cope with the daily terrors of hospital life. In subsequent years my core beliefs were to change in significant ways, but the belief system that ultimately developed was inspired during my late teens by two professionals who were willing to ignore the general norm in both their professions that dealing with existential fear such as mine was inappropriate. (At best, ministers tended to pay hospital calls by standing at the foot of the bed, offering a brief prayer, and getting away as fast as they could. And even the most sympathetic doctors usually tried to dispel fear by furnishing specific medical information, which, from my perspective, missed the point.)

Another very different sort of sensitivity was shared with me by a prison warden who was my student in an introductory social work class. We were debating whether or not counselors in institutions should read case records before the initial contact with the client (student, prisoner, patient), and this burly, obviously experienced older official told us that before he ever looked at a prisoner's record, he talked with the man and asked to hear his story without the influence of prior assessments. "I can get a feeling about the person that way—what he thinks and believes," he explained. "I can find out if we can really be of any help to him."

In a similar way, the volunteers for the hospice organization I once worked for were always on the lookout for openings into the existential beliefs of patients. Because they were in the home several times a week, frequently for several hours at a time, their only goal being supportive companionship, they often had access to private thoughts and fears with which patients might not wish to burden their families and an opportunity to reinforce the beliefs with which patients were confronting death.

Summary

In this chapter I have suggested ways of including attention to core beliefs in traditional practice methods. I have also noted that much mental health practice takes place in nontraditional settings, where opportunities for existential conversations may arise unexpectedly but where interventions have special force, occurring during times of disequilibrium and crisis as they may.

I do not contend that incorporating attention to spiritual concerns is easy, and I do not advocate this approach for all clients; a majority of my own clients over the years would have had no interest in existential questions of any kind. It is for that handful of souls, not only believers but also questers, if you will, that I am putting forth this plea for more serious attention to their search for meaning in their lives. I am also suggesting that such clients may be more numerous than a surface evaluation would indicate.

Chapter Ten

Answering Our Existential Questions

We are now ready to return to the questions that I suggested are raised by the belief systems discussed in Chapter One, questions with which each of us tries to organize our own personal chaos and reduce our existential angst. We will see if we can identify underlying belief systems and explore how existential questions influenced the direction of the interventions. I want to emphasize again that if we have unconsciously absorbed the beliefs of the people around us, we may be unaware that we have a belief system at all and unaware too that there are alternative ways of coping with life. Each of the questions discussed here will seem sensible to the person asking it, and other approaches to life will seem wrong, silly, ignorant, or even evil—a testimonial to the ferocity and the synergy of our belief systems.

As illustration of the kinds of situations a counselor might confront, I will present fictional cases (composites of persons I have known), including assessment and intervention strategies for each belief system. Do not take this compartmentalization too literally; in reality, life questions and life situations will rarely be this straightforward, but it seems necessary to highlight a somewhat unconventional methodology by keeping different belief systems separate here. As I did in presenting the different as ifs, I will divide these cases into the secular and the religious, although the distinctions can blur at times.

Secular Questions

As I have commented before, I am using the term *secular* to mean not including a concept of God.

How Can I Be Happy?

"Will" in the case that follows is a composite of several individuals, used to illustrate some of the approaches that can be helpful. In considering the existential search of a person like Will, who believes that there is no higher power of any kind, I am aware that in our culture this stance is rarely confessed to others. Mental health professionals, and especially pastors encountering an atheist, are frequently unaware of the person's deeply held skepticism, and I suppose that sometimes such persons have not really admitted it to themselves. In a case like Will's, however, atheism was reinforced by the prejudices of the religious community and was articulately specific.

I met Will shortly after his male lover of many years had walked out on him. A mutual friend referred him to me, and his despair was evident as soon as he walked into my office, shoulders bent, thin face drawn, looking like he had forgotten how to smile. Will was an accountant by profession, and it appeared that his basic stance in life was isolation, not only because of his sexual orientation but also because he was shy and introverted. After a while, when he began to share his inner thoughts with me, I learned that he perceived of himself as alone in an uncaring universe, in some sense punished both by his lover's desertion and by the AIDS epidemic, which had cut him off from previous sources of social, emotional, and sexual expression.

I acknowledged Will's profound alienation, and it occurred to me to suggest a behavioral intervention in order to give him some sense of control and to reduce his sense of helplessness. I helped him work out a schedule of positive reinforcements that might bring more pleasure into his life, lift his situational depression, and relieve his isolation. Among the pleasures that Will identified were going to the movies and photography. He agreed to invite a friend—any friend—to go with him to the movies once a week, and after much reluctance, he called the gay and lesbian office at our local university for suggestions of other activities. Gradually his desolation began to lift, and a small glimmer of hope crept into his conversations with me.

Atheism of the kind professed by Will may sometimes seem difficult to distinguish from secular humanism; the crucial variables seem to be genuine antagonism toward organized religion and cynicism about ethical absolutes. It is my impression that some people who call themselves atheists because they have trouble believing in God are really secular humanists with elaborate ethical systems stemming from their belief in the evolutionary potential of the human being, in itself an admission that life has meaning. However, I would argue that in its pure form, which I think we rarely see, atheism has no place for aesthetics or ethics except as these "meanings" provide pleasure or guarantee survival. A dramatic illustration of this lies in the sterile arts and cruel morality of the former communist countries. In this definition, atheism implies a kind of nihilism; I suspect that most therapists encountering this sort of nihilism, a reality without meaning, find themselves attempting to move the client in the direction of a more benign and more meaningful humanism in order to establish a therapeutic relationship and evoke some semblance of love and hope in the person's life. But to be logically consistent, if everything can be explained in terms of what we can perceive rather than feel or believe and can be reduced to a few simple principles, then behaviorism (stimulus-response patterns of behavior) makes sense, and the therapies that derive from behaviorism will be, as they were for Will, of particular interest. However, I should note that even the behaviorists have been forced in recent years to resort to metaphors and other nonobservable phenomena, and their ideas about the reinforcement effects of the environment and other repeatable experiences of pleasure or pain have taken on a hint of an aesthetic. Perhaps the chilly objectivity of the original methodology has been softened and humanized by experience.

What Are the Cause and the Effect?

Humanism, you will recall, is the set of beliefs that focuses on scientific understanding of human needs and desires rather than on metaphysical concepts. As the search for causes is the foundation of traditional psychotherapy, the humanist approach is used by nearly all therapists, whether they realize it or not. Furthermore, as noted earlier, humanism is so ubiquitous in our culture that it feels, not like a belief, but like "common sense."

An irritated school counselor referred Judy to me. "I don't think she pays any attention to her son," the counselor reported, "and I really don't think she wants him around." Judy turned out to be a small, slender woman who looked like a gray-haired hippie. Her lined face betrayed her age even though, when we met, she was wearing a short leather skirt and a tight cotton sweater. She arrived in my office the very picture of resistance, defying me to be helpful, obviously not willing to tell me one word more than I could pry out of her with direct questioning.

"Why did the school want you to see me?" I asked her. She replied that her son Jack had been in continual trouble at school. "I don't blame him," she observed sulkily. "School sucks."

When I agreed that sometimes schools seem more like prisons than anything else, I could see her face soften for an instant.

"What would you like for Jack?" I asked. "Tell me about him."

"He's okay," she said defensively, "but he's a lot like me. I hated school too, but I was such a coward that I didn't tell anybody. I just went and was bored to death. At least he has the nerve to stay away."

It was not long before I got a clear picture of a young boy caught between a traditional, somewhat strict father whom he saw only on occasional weekends and a divorced mother who longed for her own adolescence and secretly applauded her son's misbehavior. Finally one day I said to her, "What could you do now to be the person you wish you had been when you were fourteen like Jack?"

Tears came to her eyes. "Too late," she observed stoically. "I've made my bed and all that."

"Tell me about the bed you made," I suggested. Judy then described a bitter and depleting divorce settlement that left her supporting herself as a nurse's aide, but she felt she had won because she got custody of Jack.

"When you look into the future, what do you hope for yourself?" I persisted.

"I want to be independent, to run my own life, not to have other people . . . " she paused and narrowed her eyes, "*men . . .* " she added significantly, "tell me what to do."

Judy came to understand that at some level she wanted to relive her youth through her son, and when we explored that feeling, she revealed that she had chafed under the restrictions of her own overly strict parents, married at seventeen, and then found herself miserable for the next decade or so "doing the wife and mother bit," as she put it. Her rebellion began with her discovery of the women's movement. All of her pent-up rage was poured into her conventional marriage, and without conscious recognition of what was happening, she began copying teenage clothes and mannerisms. Finally she defied her husband by taking a job as an attendant in a nursing home and going to adult education classes at night. Not surprisingly, the marriage broke down, and Judy and Jack were now living in subsidized housing while she fought for continuing custody of the boy.

As old as Judy was, she had not yet accomplished one of the primary tasks of adolescence—she had not yet formed a stable self-image. And as tends to happen with adolescents who are struggling with their roles and values, Judy and I eventually got into conversations about the meaning of human existence. ("What do you think life is all about?" I suppose I asked her at some point.) She had given it a lot of thought and seemed to be touched and pleased to have an audience for her musings. She had no sense of any supernatural force in the world but did feel a moral compulsion to "clean up the shit" caused by greed and selfishness (among other things). Gradually a somewhat coherent belief system began to emerge, one that gave substance to her restlessness and direction to her ambitions. She did not believe in conventional ideas of God but thought that maybe "something" was expected of her. "I don't know what," she observed reflectively. "I guess I believe in the golden rule and stuff like that." She thought maybe "God," whatever that meant, was around in things like art and nature.

Eventually Judy was able to stop encouraging Jack's delinquency, and with the understanding of her own motivation came a willingness to allow Jack to live with his father. The artistic sensibility that had suggested itself in her youthful wardrobe was enhanced when she bought a sewing machine and began designing and making her own clothes. When last I heard from her, she had enrolled in nursing school and had to some extent managed to reduce the size of the chip on her shoulder.

It seems to me that Judy was a classic humanist in that even though she could not buy into any religion ("all that hocus-pocus"), she had a deep sense of human connectedness and mutual responsibility. She loved her nursing courses because the explanations made sense, and she felt anchored in their consistency and believability. Her relationship with her patients also gave her an outlet for love feelings, an important aspect of her new adult awareness. Her angst was reduced by her increasing ability to solve her own problems herself. I hope that the rambling philosophical conversations she and I engaged in built an ideological framework that will be useful for her over a long period of time.

In considering intervention strategies, it is worthwhile noticing that humanists are often passionate advocates for both love and justice—not "eye for an eye" justice but rather the sort of justice understood in our sense of fairness. Love and justice in this belief system are crucial to our relationships, and the word *relationship* is central for humanists, especially emotional relationships between human beings. Many of the theories of personality development and personal growth strategies of the humanistic psychologies stem from this understanding: such concepts as Carl Rogers's notion of "unconditional positive regard" (1961).

I have found that in addition to acknowledging the power of love, seeking out artistic metaphors is an especially important tool in the search for meaning in a humanist's life because they are suggestive windows onto realities outside immediate experience—wide-angle lenses broadening the individual's focus, so to speak. I think the best humanistic metaphors can be found in the arts of the past four hundred years, the towering centuries when Beethoven and the Impressionists and Shakespeare were freed from the constraints of a too-literal religiosity and reality unfolded for the Western world in luminous creations of art and music and literature. Some of the most recent humanistic therapies have begun to use these metaphors in their systems of interaction—one of my favorites consists of spreading out dozens of art postcards and asking group members to choose three or four and explain why they like them. Within the humanistic framework, the arts offer hints of our essential unity and a road into the unconscious mind, paralleled only by dreams; they are, in a sense, waking dreams.

For someone like Judy, a person with strong aesthetic sensibilities, the experiencing of these astonishing visions was incorporated into the therapy: an in-depth consideration of concerts, art exhibits, and poetry readings uncovered metaphors of importance to both of us and enriched the symbolic content of the therapeutic sessions. When I first knew her, Judy's chaotic personal life was projected onto her son. By the time we terminated, she was grounded in her work and in the life of her active imagination.

How Can I Experience Unity with the Higher Consciousness?

As I was trying to think of case examples for this life question, I found myself stumped. I have known of individuals who took up the practice of meditation, either in a Buddhist center or with the Transcendental Meditation program, and I myself spent five days near Washington, D.C., experiencing the power of a silent retreat. I also learned a variety of meditation techniques from Francis Geddes during a healing workshop and from John Biersdorf during an introduction to body therapies, but I could not for the life of me recall a client whose core belief involved an interest in the kind of mysticism we are calling the "quest for unity." So instead I propose to offer the story of a client who discovered her own kind of meditation as a tool for tolerating intense psychological pain. I am aware that in some ways this resembles the relaxation techniques taught by behavioral therapists, but I think its peculiarly religious focus gives it a somewhat different slant. She combined an altered state of consciousness—a sort of self-hypnosis—with a deeply felt sense of a "healing presence" and thus was able to bear the loosening of her ego boundaries that led to the recovery of long-repressed memories. I leave you to decide whether or not this was a religious solution—it did not involve any doctrines but did take place in church and did involve a higher power of some kind.

I first heard about Ruthanne through the pastor of a local Methodist church whom she had sought out for counseling. "She needs more intensive help than I'm prepared to give her," he told me, "but she insists that she will only talk about her problems here at the church." He offered to lend me an office if I would come to the church to see her. She was a tall, somewhat disheveled redhead with the most tired-looking eyes I had ever seen; she looked decades older than her forty-some years. The tears came minutes after she began to tell me her story in the little church-school office. She had recently begun to have memories of severe sexual abuse by her father, something she had repressed for years. "I can't remember details," she reported hesitantly, wringing her hands and holding her body stiff and straight. "But if I close my eyes and meditate, I feel as though I can get through this." We began carefully to explore her sense of this healing presence. A few months earlier, when her personal life had become complicated and difficult, she evolved for herself a way of meditating in front of a small altar she set up in her bedroom. Using the candle on the altar as a point of focus, she discovered how to empty her mind of obsessive thoughts and simply "float" with the visual image of the candle. She found that feelings of aloneness tended to dissolve and a peaceful sense of support and love would take their place during those times. However, one day while she was meditating, a vague memory of a sexual encounter with her father, which had apparently occurred when she was about five years old, intruded into her thoughts. While she was by her altar, she didn't feel frightened, but if she let herself think about it later, the memory seemed overwhelming. She feared that more memories would flood in if she let them, and even though she didn't know what their content would be, she was sure that they would be devastatingly upsetting.

Ruthanne and I examined why she wanted to be seen in the church building and talked together about the support she got from the church itself. Together we walked around the building to see if we could find a space with more meaning for her than the church-school office. Eventually we came upon an alcove off the main sanctuary that she identified as a place she particularly loved. "Would you like to meet with me here?" I asked her. "We could do it once a week for the next three months or so, and then we'll see how you are feeling. We can go as slowly as is comfortable for you, and we can sit in silence together before every session." Ruthanne and I met in that little alcove for more than six months. Our sessions evolved a shape that we scrupulously honored: we bowed our heads before we began talking and observed a few moments of silence; then, at Ruthanne's initiative, she would quietly tell me what she had learned during the week. The "learnings" came in the form of images during her meditation. "It is as though I'm allowed to see what I can bear and no more than that." Over time the images became more explicit, more terrifying, and more complete. But oddly enough, they never occurred during her times with me; she brought them "ready-made" from her small altar at home. Finally, in one of the most abrupt terminations I can remember, one day she announced that she was done. "I've remembered it all," she said. "I'll be okay." I admit to being somewhat skeptical, but when we talked after church a few months later, she told me she had continued her meditation practices and did not wish to go any further with psychotherapy.

I am convinced that many people in our Western culture are asking about mystical and meditative practices and do not know very much about them. The whole New Age phenomenon is a reflection of the desire people feel to be connected to a philosophy that reflects their paranormal experiences. We mental health professionals are beginning to explore the seriousness of a quest for inner peace that implies taking alternate realities, and especially what I have earlier referred to as a "tilt toward unity," seriously. Pastors and mental health professionals are beginning to learn and practice several forms of meditation themselves, if only to have a basis for dialogue with persons for whom this is an important opening to other possible realities, but even so I am frequently surprised by the suspicion I encounter in my colleagues on both religious and mental health fronts over meditative practices, as if prayer were not a form of meditation or as if hypnotism were not a historically important tool in psychotherapy. But I sense that this attitude is changing and that there is new openness to mysticism in its many forms within our mutual communities.

Religious Questions

You will remember that I defined religion as any system imputing a definition of universal meaning to life, usually but not always implying some sort of deity.

How and Where Do I Encounter God?

What I am calling "personal salvation" is a particularly Christian belief system, and we need only encounter the various forms of Christian broadcasting to realize how widespread it is. In this country, where Christianity is the majority belief system, this concept must be understood and appreciated by therapists of all backgrounds if they hope to address the core beliefs of a large number of their clients. I urge those non-Christian therapists who find the concept offensive to refer the client to a more sympathetic professional rather than simply bracket it off.

My relationship with Rhonda gave me particular satisfaction as her therapist because strengthening her beliefs had such a dramatic effect on her life. "I've made a lifework out of being a psychotherapy patient," she once commented to me. She had been referred by her priest, and we would usually get together at an outdoor picnic table during her lunch hour—neutral territory for someone who had been in too many professional offices. "I've been through them all," she noted with amusement. "None of them took." It turned out that at the age of thirty-eight, Rhonda had experienced most of the popular therapies of the past several decades, but in spite of the efforts of these psychological interventions, she remained depressed, angry, and often suicidal. "I'm too smart for them, I think," she observed wearily. "I can always pick out the flaws in their reasoning."

"Your priest seems very concerned about you," I noted in response. "Has he been helpful?"

The answer to that question was contained in a description of how Rhonda became involved with the church in the first place. Several years earlier, she had felt an odd urge to begin to attend a Catholic church near her home. "But I wanted to hide in a corner so no one would see me—I was so embarrassed to be there," she told me later, but in spite of her embarrassment, she continued to attend sporadically. Then one spring day she was transfixed by what seemed to her a spiritual revelation—an odd, intense insight. She was walking up the steps to her house and noticed nearby lilacs in bloom. "It hit me like a blow on the head that those lilacs couldn't be accidental, that something had 'caused' them to be there. I stood and stared at them for a long time, and afterward everything seemed different." She felt dazed, disconnected from reality, and above all convinced of the existence of God.

When she hesitantly told a Catholic friend about her experience, it seemed connected with her having been led to attend church, and he suggested that she talk with the priest at that church, a person she already liked and admired. (In some cases, referral to a minister turns out to be appropriate.) The priest gently helped Rhonda think through her lifelong sense of connection with a "higher power" (an image of God or more specific Christian images would take longer to develop) and begin to practice some spiritual disciplines: daily prayer, regular reading of church classics, keeping a spiritual journal, attending Mass. Over the course of time, her faith began to supplant her ferocious and frightening doubts, but once in a while the doubts would overwhelm her, and on one of those occasions, she called me—she had heard about me from the priest, with whom I had had a referral relationship for some time.

"God and I have had a falling out," she explained. "Father says you'll be good for me because you're so sure of what you believe." We discussed my beliefs briefly and discovered that the question for her was not what to believe but *how*. So over our sandwiches we would again and again explore her doubts and her relationship with God, especially since God had become a projective target for all her disappointments with human beings—God as an object of transference, so to speak. By then Rhonda knew more about transference in the abstract than most people do, and it did not take long for her to begin to see that she was doing to God what she had done to all those other therapists. "I guess I'm also smarter than God," she said to me with an ironic smile one day.

Rhonda's spiritual life was no more consistent than any other aspect of her life, but gradually she stopped taking out her anger and skepticism on God, began spiritual direction with a nun from a local convent, and attended a yearly retreat. Though her depression still disabled her from time to time, her life assumed a direction and purpose that helped her ride out the hard times, and the memory of those lilacs bolstered her faith when it began to lag.

In my own psychotherapy practice, I have encountered a number of persons who have had sudden conversion experiences such as Rhonda's. Invariably, these people are surprised (astonished even) because the experience is unlooked for and unexpected. They are confused because it does not fit into the framework of their regular lives and concerned by the thought that they might be "crazy." They come to me because word is out that I will listen nonjudgmentally. The experience I am describing is similar to the unitive experience Gerald May talks about, though there is usually some sort of content, even if the content comes afterward. It is also different from being "born in the spirit," which is a structured experience within the charismatic religious communities. For every person I have talked with who has had such an experience, I presume pastors will have talked with a hundred. Its commonness makes it of particular interest, I should think, to both pastors and therapists.

I will talk at greater length about criteria for distinguishing revelational experience from psychosis later. In Rhonda's case, the consistency, the coherence, and above all the positive effect on her everyday life were persuasive. Persons like Rhonda greatly benefit from what is called "spiritual direction." She had begun a spiritual journey, and, as Gerald May observes, the need for direction on a spiritual journey increases as the journey progresses, unlike therapy, where the goal is eventually to eliminate the need for a therapist. The person on a spiritual journey is not "sick" and thus does not need to be "healed," however tempting it may be to approach the experience in this way (May, 1982).

Spiritual direction has been described in various ways. At the Shalem Institute for Spiritual Formation in Washington, D.C., which I had occasion to visit during my studies, it is described as follows: "Spiritual direction, sometimes referred to as spiritual guidance or spiritual friendship, is an ongoing relationship in which one person (the directee), desirous of being attentive to his or her spiritual life, meets with another person (the director) on a regular basis (approximately once a month), specifically for the purpose of becoming more attuned to God's Presence in order to respond more fully to that Presence in all of life."

The Shalem staff also suggests the following distinctions between spiritual direction and therapy: "In general it might be said that therapy and counseling deal primarily with problem areas of one's life and attempt to bring healthy resolution to issues. Spiritual direction is concerned with finding and responding to God (in the midst of pain or disorder as well as in the rest of life). Problem-issue solving is not the primary focus of direction."

Persons who have had revelational experiences are frequently disoriented by them. I am not sure that we understand psychologically what happens to their previous belief systems, but it is important that mental health professionals respect the integrity of the experiences and help individuals merge them into their lives.

Who Shall We Become?

Cocreationism is a sort of counterculture within the religious world, rarely talked about in specifically religious terms and somewhat out of favor in contemporary religious politics. But I am convinced that it offers lovely opportunities for the small group of people who are drawn to it, and I have no doubt that it will survive in new forms, whatever may come of the intentional communities of the 1960s and 1970s. I think Terry and others of his generation exemplify the types of individuals who can live out and revitalize this belief system.

Terry was an almost prototypical Vietnam survivor, bearded and shabby, with an indirect, hesitant manner. Since returning from that war, he had drifted between jobs and between relationships with women, and sometimes a sense of self-doubt nearly over-whelmed him, causing him to find a counselor to talk with. He told me that he felt betrayed by his country and by his own sense of patriotism, seduced into giving up his youth for worse than no rea-son at all, and left without direction or ambition, disillusioned and cynical.

I learned that Terry had grown up in an active Baptist family and still felt some sense of longing for the church life of his child-hood but resented the church's support for the war and had the sense that he was an alien presence in his family's life. Zeroing in on what seemed to be nostalgia for his religious childhood, I sug-gested that Terry begin attending our local Quaker meeting. He immediately loved it.

"At first," he later reported, "I just enjoyed the quietness and the friendliness of the people. But then I started listening to what they were saying when someone would speak—they speak only when they think they have a special understanding of some kind—and then I began staying after the regular meeting for the discus-sion period. I was amazed when I realized that here was a whole organized group of people who didn't believe in war of any kind." The Quakers befriended Terry in their unintrusive way, including him in church activities and finally in social justice activities. Three years after his first visit, Terry became a member and recognized that his life had developed new meaning and new content.

In my own experience, I have found adults of Terry's genera-tion to be most affected by radical religious philosophies (though in some sense all religious systems are radical in the beginning) and most attracted to communities like the Quakers, radical Catholics such as the Catholic Workers, the Word of God community in the

Midwest, convents, monasteries, and intentional communities like the Church of the Savior in Washington, D.C., the Mennonites, the Mormons—as incomplete as this list is, it is a surprisingly large group.

Cocreationists, by their very convictions, need to find communities of like-minded people. Conventional churches rarely meet their needs. These people express despair and loneliness when they are alone with their passion and their visions, and there is great joy in the realization that there are organized schools of thought and organized places of action that address their condition. The synergy developed when cocreationists organize communities is a force for good that is, in my judgment, desperately needed in a world of ethical entropy and scientific nihilism.

It is my belief that the radical 1960s survived in the religious communities of the 1970s and 1980s both in North America and in the Third World, but many have fallen on harder times in the 1990s. I think we owe it to ourselves and our clients and parishioners to be informed about them—to visit them, to know their members, and to retain an open mind about their objectives. As I will explain later, I think there is far too great a tendency in our professions to call any group that deviates from the norm a "cult" and perhaps not tendency enough to be familiar with positive experiments in community living so as to be able to provide alternatives to the destructive ones.

What Is God's Word for Me?

I have heard the story I am about to tell in many forms from many people. I could substitute some nonreligious cult for the one described here, but the basic impulse of adolescents to find their own belief system, different from their family's, is so common as to be nearly universal.

"Our children have deserted us," Mr. and Mrs. H. reported to the Reverend G. "They went to hear Billy Graham and—you're not going to believe this—they went down in front of all those people and took the pledge! Pastor, they've been raised in this church, they went to Sunday school, they were confirmed—what were they thinking of? Now they're telling us we need to be born again and that we're not good Christians. We tell them if they're going to be so insulting, they need never come into our house again."

It had become a familiar story for the Reverend G. The big Billy Graham convention had attracted a lot of local attention, and several of his Baptist parishioners had told him that they had renewed their commitment to Christ. But the two H. teenagers were sensitive and intense church members, and he was not surprised to hear that the experience had had a big impact on them. It reminded him of the tent revivals in his own little town in the South and of his own conversion experience, how excited he was the day he "took Jesus into his heart." In those days and in that place, people were more accepting of emotional conversions, but still, that moment had set him on the course that had directed the rest of his life.

"Well, folks," he ventured cautiously to the H.'s, "people have to decide for themselves what they believe. You can plow the field, so to speak, but God plants the seeds." Yet even as he tried to explain this, he knew that the H. youngsters might well be beginning a life of faith very different from their parents', and it occurred to him that he was going to have a hard time convincing the parents that this might be a good thing. "I guess the moral is, be careful what you teach your children," he told me later with a smile. "They might take you seriously."

The belief that Jesus Christ is still alive in the world takes the idea of alternate realities to an extreme form. This is, of course, a fundamental premise of traditional Christianity—the "good news" of the Gospel. Whether accepting of it or not, no pastor or therapist can have a truly open conversation with a conservative Christian without dealing with this belief. However we explain it, many Christians have had what they are convinced is an encounter with Jesus. The Gospels imply that an encounter with Jesus and belief in the literal truth of the Bible are essential, and a large group of Christian fundamentalists accepts this, as Muslim fundamentalists accept a literal reading of the Koran and Jewish fundamentalists accept a literal interpretation of the Torah.

I am not discounting problems with proselytizing such as the H.'s were encountering with their children. The Reverend G. was sympathetic with their frustration, if not hopeful that their children would change. All over the world, boundary-protecting fundamentalists of various persuasions are standing guard at the ramparts. Because their boundaries are frequently cast in cognitive concrete, they not surprisingly lack the flexibility to deal creatively with ideas other than their own. I am only suggesting that we be generous enough to acknowledge that ours is not the only way to experience reality and to appreciate the clarity and nonambiguity of fundamentalist theology when it is generous and undefensive, as many people have experienced it with the Billy Graham organization and as I have experienced it with a number of fundamentalist students, clients, and friends.

Also there is a certain justification to the fundamentalists' conviction that they are under attack; one only needs to try to write about them without becoming sarcastic to be aware of how scornful the larger culture is of these beliefs. We are being as dogmatic as they are, I would suggest, when we make fun of their experience of God.

Fundamentalists of whatever persuasion are concerned, above all, with their scriptures. Every existential question, in the West at least, is perceived to be answered by the Bible, the Koran, or the Torah. I have to confess that I have been surprisingly convinced by some of the arguments fundamentalists make for a literal acceptance of various scriptures, even though I have trouble with their legalistic rules for life. But whether or not we accept their reading of it, we can enjoy the passion with which they encounter the Author of their sacred books.

Summary

Although mental health professionals practice in a wide variety of settings and address a wide variety of concerns, every mental health encounter has the basic components of contact, relationship building, assessment, goal setting, intervention, evaluation, and termination. At each phase of mental health treatment, if the therapist is willing to be "transparent" to the client and is able to incorporate concern with core beliefs in his or her interviewing and listening repertory, existential assumptions can add a forward-looking dimension to the therapeutic arsenal.

The various religious and psychological belief systems we have described offer modes of intervention that can answer the life questions raised by the core beliefs we have been describing. They can help both clients and therapists face the future in ways that merely dissecting the past cannot do, and they offer relief from the existential anxiety and chaos inherent in the human condition.

Part Two

—

RELIGION AND MENTAL HEALTH

Chapter Eleven

The Case for Religion

I think that a counselor or therapist, when confronted with a very religious client, may have an almost irresistible urge to analyze the "healthiness" of the religion. Setting aside the argument that other people's religions are impossible to evaluate objectively, I would also like to argue that it is not fruitful to do so. We have observed that private belief systems are clung to with passion; it is equally true that people are unlikely to be dissuaded from their religious convictions. Nevertheless, knowledge of various religious systems can enable us to understand the ways in which a particular religion serves the emotional and existential needs of our clients, and such knowledge can provide an additional tool for enhancing the relational and metaphorical resources with which the client faces the future.

Religions are not vague philosophies. They are above all complex cultures representing metaphysical universes. The philosopher George Santayana noted how inclusive and specific a true religion is. He observed, "An attempt to speak without speaking any particular language is not more hopeless than the attempt to have a religion that shall be no religion in particular. Thus every living and healthy religion has a marked idiosyncrasy. Its power consists in its special and surprising message and in the bias which that revelation gives to life. The vistas it opens and the mysteries it propounds are another world to live in; and another world to live in—whether we expect ever to pass wholly over into it or no—is what we mean by having a religion" (Geertz, 1973, p. 87).

It is a hypothesis of this discussion that human beings are incurably religious. Just as we unavoidably have core beliefs about reality, so too we attempt to fit those beliefs into some sort of consistent pattern. *Religion* in this sense may refer to what we mean by the conventional use of the word, or it may mean one of the secular religions: an organized belief system without a supernatural component, such as socialism, fascism, or humanism, all of which fit our definition in that they provide "a world to live in." Even science is a sort of religion, as we quickly discover in conversation with a convinced believer who insists on language and evidence grounded in experience. As the British writer Bryan Appleyard asserts, "Science now answers questions *as if* it were a religion and its obvious effectiveness means that these answers are believed to be the Truth—again *as if* it were a religion" (Appleyard, 1992, p. 214).

    I would like in this chapter to reflect on the biases about religion that I perceive within our profession and to puzzle over the question of cults, which is a legitimate concern within both the mental health and the religious worlds. Once again I will briefly but unavoidably flirt with theology, but only to tease you into some philosophical speculation about the nature of religion in general.

The Value of Traditional Religions

Whether a person's belief system is lived out in a conventional religion or in a secular philosophical framework, the impulse toward a culturally organized institution of some kind, with activities and rituals and doctrines supporting and interpreting its core beliefs, seems to be nearly ubiquitous in human society. And for a majority of people in the world, the institution that supports their beliefs is one of the traditional world religions. I would like here to examine the various ways in which institutional religion provides an organized receptacle for beliefs—in Santayana's phrase, "a world to live in." I would add parenthetically that whatever the religion, it must fulfill two functions: it must provide consistent patterns for the living out of core beliefs, and it must provide organized ceremonies in which its adherents can participate, to give them a sense of collective self and a place in the chaos of reality. (In Chapter

Twelve we will examine that most basic ceremonial activity, worship.)

The psychiatrist-theologian David Sheinkin (1986) makes a compelling argument for the unity and internal consistency of traditional religious systems, what he refers to as "spiritual paths." He notes that many of them have been refined over thousands of years and that they have stood the test of time as well as any human system. But he observes that today, with a deluge of information available about many different religious and spiritual systems, there is a great temptation to pick and choose bits and pieces from several that seem attractive, without awareness of how the pieces fit together to make a unified whole. He argues that this method will not lead to spiritual growth because "if one does not follow the system in its entirety one loses the whole inner harmony that it seeks to establish" (p. 4). In this sense, a spiritual path resembles Santayana's world to live in, and, as Sheinkin says, "it is possible to pick any one of these [spiritual] paths and, irrespective of which one is picked, to arrive at the same destination" (p. 3).

Traditional world religions have particular value in providing worlds to live in precisely because they have had centuries of internal experience—experiments, critiques, new insights, mistakes, and successes—with which to provide corrective substance to their beliefs and practices. It is my purpose to make a case for churches, synagogues, temples, and mosques themselves—whatever organizational structure a particular religion inhabits—and to suggest criteria for separating genuine religion from the destructive cults that come and go on a regular basis. But it is important to stress again that endorsement of "healthy" religion is not the province of mental health professionals; as this discussion will indicate, this is at best a murky area of inquiry.

It has been my experience that my professional colleagues and friends over the years have not been well informed about the ways in which religions are organized. To the extent that we as a group have not ourselves participated in church life, we tend to know about churches primarily through their anomalies and public controversies rather than through the astonishing range of their positive organizations and activities. In a tartly worded essay, the anthropologist Mary Douglas points out that professionals were startled by the resurgence of traditional religious forms all over the world, having confidently predicted the weakening influence of religion in the modern era, because "their eyes were glued to those conditions of modern life identified by Weber as antipathetic to religion" (Douglas and Tipton, 1982, p. 25). She notes that we pay attention to religious practices that support our own beliefs and that most social scientists find personal and private forms of religious worship more appealing than collective, ritualized systems. For this reason, many intellectuals have been fascinated by religious observances of the East—Hinduism and Buddhism in particular—and consequently have failed to assess the important resurgence of fundamentalism in Christianity, Judaism, and Islam. In Douglas's words, "the wise men missed what was happening in the West because they were gazing toward the East" (p. 28).

Much of what seems objectionable to outsiders about organized religion has to do with its status as a system. It is all too easy to forget that without ongoing, formal systemic structure, most, if not all, religions would have long ago disappeared. Their value as refiners of the human instinct for worship and awe would not be available to us today, and we would each be thrown back on our own feeble efforts to express the inexpressible; the already alarming tendency for cults and black magic rituals to proliferate would run rampant, and we would be left spiritually naked, prey to every grandiose messiah or spiritual magician who came along. Indeed, this seems already to be happening.

One of the primary tasks of a system, as we discussed earlier, is to perpetuate itself. This requires the maintenance of boundaries (who may belong, what the rituals are, what the rules are), the distribution of energy (what members and clergy do and where the money comes from), and clarity of purpose (creeds, form of worship, scripture and prayer books), among other variables. Traditions extending over time are particularly important for the maintenance of a religious system whose life is not decades but centuries, and modifications must be made gradually. This gives many religions the appearance of being rigid and unresponsive to contemporary conditions and knowledge. I mention these technical aspects of system organization to address a common objection to organized religion: that it is too stultifying, not respectful of individuality, not inspiring enough, in some cases too "old-fashioned." But according to the sociologists Roger Finke and Rodney Stark (1992), when there is too much newness, a distinctive religious system will dissolve altogether, its power and traditional mysticism evaporating into its efforts to be relevant. As they put it, "Humans want their churches to be sufficiently potent, vivid, and compelling so that they can offer them rewards of great magnitude. People seek a religion that is capable of miracles and that imparts order and sanity to the human condition" (p. 275).

The theologian Paul Tillich has argued that "genuine religion" must interpret human experience and especially what he calls "revelatory experience," meaning experience outside the realm of the sensory, in such a way as to lead to personal wholeness and social integration (Tillich, 1951). He assumes that religion stems from the experience of an essential unity, a "ground of being," rather than being the source of this experience. In other words, religion does not create encounters with God (or with a cosmic unity that may not be specifically identified as God) but rather results from such encounters. According to Tillich, the symbols, rituals, and doctrines of religion are attempts to organize such encounters and should return the worshiper to an experience of that unity. All world religions began with an experience of mystery on the part of a charismatic individual (Moses, Jesus, Confucius, the Buddha, Muhammad) and the subsequent codification and interpretation of that experience by others. The religion thus created is significant to the extent that it breathes life into intimations of existential meaning already present in the culture—we can see that Moses' encounter with Yahweh had a particular impact on a migrant refugee population with an already well developed sense of their own powerful God and that the intersection of Greek and Hebrew cultures provided fertile ground for the emergence of early Christianity. We cannot imagine Islam originating elsewhere than on the Arabian peninsula, with its tribal customs and severe living conditions, or Buddhism being born far from the sophisticated Hindu culture that spawned it.

"Wholeness," as Tillich speaks of it, is frequently invoked by both theologians and psychologists. It is sometimes hard for mental health professionals to see how fundamentalist religions in particular can lead to anything remotely resembling wholeness because the rigid boundaries and severe injunctions of many of these religions seem harsh and punitive. But to repeat a thesis offered in Chapter Two, religion often provides structure for an otherwise disorganized personality or, more significant these days, for a threatened and beleaguered group. A religion that would seem harsh and punitive to someone with a flexible superego and a reliable emotional support system may offer welcome strength, companionship, and structure to an impulse-ridden individual living in a chaotic environment. Furthermore, personally disorganized individuals are likely to seek rigid support structures whether or not religions provide them—hence the appeal of gangs with stern initiation and membership rules or cults in which a charismatic leader issues orders and defines reality out of his own delusional system. How much better it is to find one's way into well-regulated and socially accepted fundamentalist religions, with leadership accountable to the larger group and defined and established expectations and ideals validated by historical experience. The wholeness thus promoted might not be appropriate for persons at the other end of the emotional spectrum, but that merely confirms that there are many recipes for wholeness.

The integration and interpretation of revelatory experience are not the only criteria for the discernment of genuine religion. As we noted earlier, the anthropologist-psychologist Ernest Becker has based a philosophy of religion on the human being's natural and inevitable fear of death. He sees the fear of death as a direct and deliberate contrast to Freud's emphasis on sexuality and considers genuine religion as leading to an understanding of our mortality rather than the denial that he suggests motivated the Freudians. (Freud indeed argued that religion was a form of denial.) As Becker

(1973, p. 124) puts it, "In order to move from *scientific* creatureliness to *religious* creatureliness, the terror of *death* would have to replace sex, and inner *passivity* would have to replace obsessive Eros, the drive of the creature." This somewhat bleak allegation points out that rather than basing our psychology on our instinctive drives, religion suggests to us that our basic concern is our mortality. In other words, Becker's conception of the role of religion presents a challenge built on the conviction that whatever psychotherapy has to offer is in the end limited by human mortality and by what he grimly refers to as "creation as a nightmare spectacular taking place on a planet that has been soaked for hundreds of millions of years in the blood of all its creatures" (p. 283). He asserts that to come to terms with this stark reality, the "heroic" person must ultimately depend on genuine religion.

The word *passivity* will strike a harsh note with many modern professionals, especially with many feminists, and seems to be at odds with much of the "empowerment" movement in psychology. I have no argument with which to make more acceptable a concept absolutely central to most religions, except to note that passivity docs *not* mean helplessness. Gerald May (1982) has addressed this issue by distinguishing between helplessness and what he calls "willingness." He has written extensively on the distinction between attempting "to control . . . and manipulate existence," which he calls "willfulness," and "willingness," meaning "the surrendering [of] one's self-separateness" (p. 6). He says of this distinction, "Willingness notices [the wonder of life] and bows in some kind of reverence to it. Willfulness forgets it, ignores it, or at its worst, actively tries to destroy it" (p. 6).

An image of passivity that comes to mind is the seated, cross-legged Buddha, eyes closed, smiling, with open hands resting on relaxed knees, waiting. It is the basic stance of apophatic prayer, which I will discuss in Chapter Twelve. This stance assumes a beneficent unity, a healing presence (either within or without) that is available to the extent that we are receptive to it. It is impossible to overstress this point. The essential religious stance in life, no matter what the religion, is the assumption that within ourselves or within creation there exists a capacity for psychological and physical self-healing, as well as a yearning—a talent, even—for what we are calling "wholeness," which originates in some sort of universal goodness. This is not essentially different from humanistic psychology's basic premise, and I have no doubt that Carl Rogers in particular brought his background as a pastor to his original concepts (see his classic work, *On Becoming a Person*, 1961).

Discerning Cults

From a mental health perspective, the nature of the religions within which we and our clients live should be of central interest because, as someone has wryly put it, the trouble with not believing in *something* is that one will then believe in *anything*. And *anything* in this context can mean all sorts of odd and destructive cults and gangs and sects; we can observe the dangers of such cults, both socially and psychologically, on the streets of our cities and in the headlines of our newspapers.

I want to make some distinctions between cults and religions. It has been correctly observed that most religions began as cults, if by this we mean a belief system originated by a charismatic leader such as Jesus, Muhammad, Moses, or the Buddha. Even secular religions such as socialism and fascism are associated with individual leaders. So the identification of an organized religious group with a particular leader does not necessarily tell us anything about its value. Furthermore, sometimes groups that are unpopular and even persecuted—because their beliefs are too far outside the conventional religious wisdom of their time or because they represent a threat to contemporary authorities (the original Protestant churches being a famous example)—later become accepted and influential. This has tended to be the pattern of religious history in the Western tradition, beginning with a tiny group of Israelites who were enslaved by the Egyptians and in more recent times reflected in the United States in the stories of the Mormons, the Seventh-day Adventists, the Christian Scientists, and other groups. But a review of the past does not help the concerned observer in the present to separate the wheat from the chaff and to distinguish helpful religion from harmful cult. Especially in this era of burgeoning fundamentalisms, there is a tendency for those of us with liberal outlooks to equate rigidity with destructiveness and to assume that certainty equals fanaticism, so that it seems useful again to examine criteria for assessing religious groups.

Harmful cults do exist. During the writing of this book, people called Branch Davidians barricaded themselves within their heavily armed compound outside Waco, Texas, because their leader, David Koresh, claimed to be Jesus Christ reincarnated and believed that the forces of evil, by destroying him, would bring about the destruction of the world. The compound was indeed destroyed; the world continues to exist. Why did Koresh's followers believe him? The answer seems to be that he was a hypnotic preacher who persuaded them with his seemingly encyclopedic knowledge of the Bible. But it was not rigidity or a literal interpretation of the Bible alone that caused the malevolence of the Branch Davidians but rather a willful *misreading* that caused credulous people to accept an ultimately destructive blasphemy.

The Roman Catholic community has a formula for what in religious terminology is called "discernment"—deciding what is good and what is evil—that seems to me to offer a short and sensible set of criteria for identifying cults. It asks three questions: Is the revelation or teaching consonant with Holy Scripture (the Bible, the Koran, the Torah)? Is it consistent with the overall religious tradition? Is it joyful and illuminating? I particularly like the last question because I often detect a pursed-lipped quality to many religious heresies, a darkening of purpose rather than an illumination. Though in this country messiahs come along on a regular basis and cults seem to spring up like weeds, many so-called cults have met these discernment criteria and eventually become part of the larger religious establishment or important protesting forces within the church community, if only as new branches on an old vine.

The Danish philosopher Søren Kierkegaard suggested another criterion for discernment of harmful cults that may appeal to our liberal sensibilities but presents problems in practice. I note it here because too often this is the criterion that we, as rational intellectuals, assume is correct. Kierkegaard suggested that "the good is the opening toward new possibility and choice, the ability to face into anxiety; the closed is the evil, that which turns one away from newness and broader perceptions and experiences; the closed shuts out revelation, obtrudes a veil between the person and his own situation in the world" (Kierkegaard, [1849] 1954, p. 124). I have trouble with this description because we can easily see that many long-established religions fall short of these ideals. And it may be that the models of openness and receptivity advocated by theologians and psychotherapists would, for many of our clients, be destructively permissive and vague. "I want someone to tell me what to believe," says the overwhelmed widow. "If you can't accept that, then don't talk to me about religion." Her world is already a jumble; at the least she wants surety at church. The Amish, with their rigid boundaries and backward stance in the world, qualify as a cult personifying the sort of evil described by Kierkegaard, yet I doubt if very many people would consider the Amish evil.

Fortunately, at their best, even when closed and doctrinaire, all the major religions stress loving relationships and socially integrative behavior, and these are usually cited as the criteria determining their beneficence. I am merely asking professionals to consider the purposes served by religious boundary protection and to be somewhat broad-minded in assessing what is meant by "loving relationships": even if the love exists solely within a relatively small group and excludes outsiders, is that not better than no love at all?

Once again I can imagine objections to some religions as precisely "turning away from newness and broader perceptions." Especially if fundamentalism in particular is defined as a "return to the fundamentals of the faith," which in the three Western religions means a return to their scriptures, then Kierkegaard's definition would seem to condemn all such religions as evil. But my own sense is that the historic religions ebb and flow over time, sometimes being adventurous and creative (and risking the ire of their own conservatives, as happened after the Second Vatican Council in the Roman Catholic Church) and sometimes pulling back and shoring up their boundaries so that the religion is not altogether assimilated into the larger culture.

Having referred to religions at their best, I want to digress for a moment to say a word about religions at their worst. An unavoidable problem confronted by all religious groups is the fact that there is no supreme arbiter (in this world at least) to determine the authenticity of the claims of various leaders. As more than one cynic has noted, "Any fool can call himself a Christian" (or a Muslim, or a Jew, or a Buddhist). As a Christian, my hackles are raised by remarks such as "How can you believe in a religion that promotes the terrible violence in Northern Ireland?" My response is, "The Irish promote the violence in Northern Ireland, and if they use the name of Christianity, they are being blasphemous, but neither I nor any other Christian can prevent them from doing that." If I were Muslim, I am sure I would be equally offended by high-minded critiques of "Muslim" terrorism. Crazy groups barricading themselves behind caches of high explosives in the name of religion should be seen to represent only their own psychoses, not the religion whose names they cavalierly commandeer.

We can observe that to the extent that an organized religion encourages warfare, as most of the major religions have at one time or another, they are bowing to the destructive influences that inevitably surface from time to time in any large, heterogeneous group existing over long periods. We might rather be surprised that their core beliefs and practices persist through the centuries despite persistent human aggressiveness and that in any religion at any time groups are advocating love of God and humanity and preaching peace—universal religious doctrines.

Chapter Twelve

Religion and Mental Health Practice

In this chapter I want to focus on several aspects of organized religion that directly influence our interaction with our clients. The first section offers observations about negative tendencies of which both mental health practitioners and clients are guilty: the ways in which we make other people's religions and churches objects of derision out of the need to protect our own. I point it up because without sensitivity to the reasons why we and our clients project and stereotype, it will be difficult to explore unfamiliar religious practices. The second and third sections are descriptions of aspects of worship that apply to all organized religions but are too seldom incorporated into our assessment and intervention strategies.

Projections and Stereotypes

The evaluation of religious systems and the discernment of cults, as discussed in Chapter Eleven, are subject to projections and stereotyping on the part of the general public, including many mental health professionals as well as many of our clients. For example, sometimes the impression of churches as instruments of oppression, rigidity, and guilt that we get from clients results from a tendency to project their own fears and angers onto the power structures with which they are involved. Of course, some churches really are oppressive, rigid, and judgmental, but probably not as many as the complaints against them would suggest. The Gestalt therapist Fritz Perls used to say, "All is projection," meaning that we interpret the external world on the basis of our own experience. The Jungian analyst Elizabeth Howes (1971) has pointed out that we find evil in our environment to the extent that we are unable to accept it in ourselves: we project our own unacceptable feelings onto the external world. Religious systems provide targets for projection too tempting for most of us to resist, posing as they do as penultimate moral arbiters.

Not only are churches targets for personal projections of all kinds, but they also are classic repositories for stereotyping. Harmful stereotypes are evaluative as well as descriptive in ways that cannot be tested for truth or falsehood. For example, "Protestants are religious, but Catholics are superstitious," or, in terms of this discussion, "Psychology is science, but religion is wishful thinking." The evaluation is made on the basis of some prejudicial standard set by the speaker without consensus or objective evidence.

Some years ago I wrote a short story about a young woman who, during a period of emotional trauma in her life, is overwhelmed by emotion during communion in an Episcopal church at Easter. In her rapture, instead of returning to her seat at the appropriate time, she remains kneeling at the altar rail and is eventually joined by an assistant minister who knows her story and stays quietly on his knees beside her until the service is over. When I asked a colleague for a critical evaluation of the story, she said she liked it but was skeptical that any minister would do such a thing. "Do you really know a minister like that?" she asked me doubtfully. When I replied that I did, I could see from the expression on her face that her stereotype of the clergy precluded sensitive, compassionate behavior of the sort I had described.

We all proceed from stereotypes of various kinds; life is too complicated to allow for critical evaluations of every unfamiliar situation. But religious institutions and clergy other than our own are peculiarly subject to stereotyping because of the emotional nature—indeed, the very survival value—of our individual belief systems. Not only do stereotypes provide comprehensive and convenient broad-brush impressions, but because they are crucial to our personal core beliefs, stereotypes are also often eagerly embraced to prove that other religious and intellectual organizations are flawed. If you doubt this (and are not one of their members), consider your own reaction to the Mormon missionaries or

Jehovah's Witnesses who come to your door. Could they offer you any evidence, no matter how persuasive, that would convince you to join them? Jewish readers, could your Christian friends convert you? Catholic readers, what do you believe about Protestant churches? Are they really "Christian"? Protestant readers, how uncomfortable does the practice of the Catholic Mass make you? Older readers, how do you feel about chanting, meditation, and yoga?

My intention is not to belittle strong boundary protection of this kind. As noted earlier, personal belief systems also need boundary protection if they are to remain viable for our mental health. And to repeat, we cannot believe all sorts of contradictory things at the same time; inevitably, we must choose. But I am arguing here that one of the challenges for the mental health profession is the benign acceptance of our own prejudices and stereotypes so that we can then suspend them in order to enter the life space of a client who has a belief system different from our own. I once heard someone use the word *vertigo* to describe how it feels when we do this, when our assumptions about reality are temporarily abrogated. We have observed that each of us lives within a core belief about reality, whether overtly religious or not, and our thoughts, dreams, plans, observations, and daily lives are based on that belief system, on that model of "the actual." It is no wonder, then, that we resist acknowledging that other core beliefs, other paradigms, might be true. At the very least, we might find ourselves doubting our own convictions; at worst, we might find ourselves converted.

Each of our core beliefs has its own boundaries, and it is a delicate balancing act to let our boundaries be transparent enough so that we can see through them and yet remain sensitive to their continuing presence without letting them obscure the view. (Note that science fiction and some popular mythology are built around ideas that are a little too frightening to consider "real." I find it interesting to imagine what would happen if alien beings really did land on the earth—maybe they already have; how uncomfortable does *that* make us feel?—or if the Shroud of Turin really did turn out to be authentic, or if the Lubavitcher Rebbe really did turn out to be the Messiah.)

Dimensions of Worship

We go to church because of what happens there, not primarily because of core beliefs of which we may or may not be aware. And what happens in church—worship—can be an important dimension of mental health because most of us have a need to express our awe and our appreciation of beauty in the face of the infinite. Much has been written about the psychology of the religious impulse, and it is not my intention to repeat those theories here. I am rather concerned with the *dimensions* of worship, our formalized relationship with the "great unknown." I want to describe some aspects of worship that partly define religious practices of whatever denomination or faith and to suggest the wide range of worship practices existing in the various religious traditions. When we later examine ways for clients to enhance their religious experiences, we will be aware of the many potentialities that exist.

Religions are practiced along continua of formal–informal, ritualized–spontaneous, democratic–authoritarian, and intellectual–emotional. You will recognize the resemblance of these continua to the structures of religious belief systems we discussed in Chapter Four, the subject-object split and unity versus duality. We will examine these concepts as they relate to five worship dimensions: prayer, ritual, metaphor, authority, and patterns of spirituality. You might well say, "So what? This is very obscure and hardly relevant to the work I do with distressed people." But if this makes any sense at all, then it follows that the way humans organize their belief systems, how they "act out" their solutions to the problems of angst and chaos and respond to their experiences of awe and beauty, provides us with important clues as to how they will confront the unknown future when they have finished their encounters with therapists and counselors.

Prayer

Someone recently asked me to define *prayer*. After thinking about it for a moment, I said, "Prayer is the mind's relationship with the infinite." That somewhat untraditional definition encompasses the wide variety of activities I include under the rubric of prayer in this discussion. In our Western religions, prayer presupposes God, but the Eastern religions pray without a personalized deity, and I consider that no less a connection with whatever is More.

The familiar stereotype of prayer is that it is a "wish list," an appeal to God rather than Santa Claus. Popular imagery portrays a small child kneeling beside a bed reciting, "I pray the Lord my soul to keep," or a soldier in a foxhole desperately bargaining for his life. But prayer, according to the definition I am using, has many forms, not petition only. The extremes of prayer can be thought of as *apophatic* (contentless meditation without any concept of deity) at one end of the scale and *kataphatic* (an image-filled encounter with a personalized deity) at the other. You may recognize our concept of unity versus duality in this description, in that the goal of apophatic prayer is a return to undifferentiated unity and the goal of kataphatic prayer is the experience of a particular, identifiable God. Apophatic prayer is characteristic of some Eastern religions and some monastic Christian sects, and kataphatic prayer is characteristic of most of the rest of us.

I would like to return to the stereotype of prayer as wish list for a moment. Most serious analyses of prayer would include petition as a legitimate form of prayer—after all, our hopes and dreams are bound to be expressed in conversations with God. But prayer has many other purposes; it can express gratitude, reverence, despair, even anger, and it frequently consists of questions and requests for guidance. In the Judeo-Christian tradition, the psalms are examples of various kinds of prayers. Deeply religious people of all traditions contend that they receive answers to their prayers in the form of internal imagery or unexpected events in their lives, and the psalms also include God's answers as part of the poetry. In most traditions there are also intercessory prayers—prayers for God's intervention on behalf of other people, institutions, or enterprises. Healing traditions (especially but not exclusively in Christian Science) are frequently based on intercessory prayer. Prayers can be private, individual, and silent, or they can be collective, formal, and spoken aloud. Some of the most beautiful collective prayers in the English language are found in the poetry of the old Book of Common Prayer of the Anglican churches, dating back to the seventeenth century. Prayers are deeply embedded in the cultures of many countries—the picture of devout Muslims on their knees five times a day dramatizes the impact that prayer has had in many parts of the world over many centuries. At its deepest level, prayer expresses devotion to God and opens a channel for God's reply.

In terms of mental health practice, I want once again to urge therapists to include consideration of clients' prayer lives in the content of the therapy. I am not alleging that this will be easy. As mentioned in Chapter Nine, we approach prayer life in the same way we approach any other sensitive and somewhat embarrassing subject—"tell me about it" is the basic stance. We could also include questions about the occasions when the person prays (prayers sometimes occur in surprising places—in the car while driving, for example, or in the bathroom), the forms prayers take (reciting scripture, singing hymns to oneself, saying the Rosary, reciting ritual prayers), how the individual feels when praying, and how answers to prayers are perceived. The purpose of these inquiries, it should be made clear, is not to interfere with the person's prayer life but rather to illuminate and enhance it, to reveal its meaning in the individual's life. Prayers can, as we asserted earlier, reflect a relationship of equal importance to object relations and as such are important to the mental health of a religious person. (Especially as people grow old and begin to lose their close relatives and friends, the relationship with God has special meaning for the devout individual.)

Ritual

Another aspect of religious practice could be thought of as the ritual dimension. Ritual is collective worship that establishes ceremonial boundaries, ranging from minimal ritual, in which worship originates spontaneously with the worshipers, to elaborately programmed services with a formal liturgy. In severely nonritualized worship, there is no set pattern for the ceremony except open time and permission for worshipers to contribute as they are inspired to do so (the Quaker model is a good example). We can also observe nonritualized worship in some forms of Buddhist meditation, among charismatic Christians, in many Christian prayer groups, and in some Protestant churches and Jewish ceremonies where the service is written by the participants. Conversely, the most ritually historical and formalized ceremonies are those practiced by such groups as traditional Muslim, Jewish, Orthodox, Catholic, Episcopal, and Lutheran congregations.

These extremes of ritual worship illustrate the subject-object split we talked about earlier. Formal liturgical worship is, by design, "objective." There are written prayers, a regular pattern of responsive readings, frequent performing of music, and behavioral components such as kneeling or prostration. The worshiper could, in a sense, mentally do something else while still participating. As many members of ritualized religions report, this is one of its disadvantages. The advantages, in addition to the beauty of the formal service, also include continuity over time and place (for example, no matter where an Orthodox Jew worships, much of the service will be familiar). In contrast, the nonritual extreme illustrates the subjective experience of God, or of unity in worship such as the Buddhist, and directly involves the subjective experience of the worshiper. For persons used to formal ritual, this can feel alarmingly unstructured, as though nothing is happening, but for worshipers with a complex inner life, unstructured worship can be deeply satisfying.

The extremes in the ritual dimension of worship also have to do with what we have labeled "diversity" and allow the expression of awe, beauty, goodness, and numinous experience in dramatic, subtle, and evanescent variety. No ritual will express the worship needs of everyone, and a number of scholars have been studying the relationship of personality types and worship preferences. From the standpoint of this discussion, it is important to stress that some form of ritual worship has been part of the human community at least since the Stone Age, and the tendency of certain intellectuals

to label religious ritual "superstitious hocus-pocus" arrogantly dis-
misses the most significant religious activity of the mass of
humankind throughout the ages, one that provides meaning, community, and comfort even into this scientific era.

Metaphor

Related to ritual, in fact a central aspect of it, is the more elusive
dimension of worship that we have been calling the metaphorical—the elliptical, the suggestive, the indirect. Conceptualizing
the unimaginable, the Wholly Other, occurs in many ways and on
many levels in organized religion. Direct experience of God is
alleged by some Sufi Muslims, Quakers, Pentecostal Christians, and
Kabbalistic Jews. At the other extreme, expressed symbols of the
inexpressible—myths, liturgies, parables, chanting, song, cathe-
drals, works of art, psalms, and poems—are metaphorical rather
than literal representations of what allegedly can be experienced
only indirectly.

The metaphorical dimension gives worship its power for most
people, in my judgment. As John Biersdorf once noted in an informal gathering, gazing on the infinite is like trying to look at a dim
star; if one looks at it directly, it disappears, but by looking slightly
to one side, one can see it. In the same way, trying to describe that
which is beyond direct human experience causes it somehow to
evaporate; there seems to be nothing there. But by recasting it into
metaphorical forms, we perceive its essence. This is, once again,
why artistic experience has such power even for the nonreligious.

Authority

A fourth dimension of worship has to do with authority. Who has
the authority to interpret human-divine intercourse? Authority in
the Western religions rests importantly with their scriptures, again
ranging from Orthodox Jews with their Talmudic studies and Christian Fundamentalists with their literal reading of the Bible at one
end of the scale to Jewish Reconstructionists and quasi-Christian

Unitarian-Universalists, who are primarily interested in the literary and sociological aspects of scripture, at the other pole.

Authority also refers to clergy, not only individual priests, pastors, imams, and rabbis but also defenders of the tradition—seminaries, councils, synods, the pope, the patriarchs, and so forth. At the other end of the scale of faith defenders, the personal extreme, we would find the Christian Protestants with their central conviction of the "priesthood of all believers" and the Reform Jews who try to adapt traditional values to contemporary needs. In the Eastern religions, authority is vested in the teachers—the gurus, the roshi, the lamas, and so forth.

Again, there are boundary protection considerations in this dimension of religion and also, very centrally, considerations of objectivity versus subjectivity: that is, it is vital that religion not be blown on the wind of excessive subjectivity lest it disappear into the vagaries of popular fashion. Though most religions accept contemporary interpretations, the central doctrines must be objectively preserved in order for the religion to persist.

Patterns of Spirituality

The theologian Urban Holmes III (1980) uses categories similar to mine but with a slightly different emphasis. He develops what he calls a "circle of sensibility," which refers to "patterns of spirituality" (p. 5). He identifies the ultimate goal of prayer, that most basic activity of worship, as a relationship between God and humanity, and he creates an image of prayer with both vertical and horizontal dimensions.

Vertically (gazing toward the infinite), Holmes suggests north and south poles of his circle of sensibility as "speculative" prayer at one extreme and "affective" prayer at the other. Speculative prayer involves "illumination of the mind"; affective prayer, "illumination of the emotions, or heart" (p. 4). We can immediately see the difference between intellectual discourses in, say, the Unitarian-Universalist tradition, in which there are sometimes lectures rather than sermons, and the "speaking in tongues" of the Pentecostals or the emotional participation of worshipers in many African-American churches. These examples show that the two extremes coexist within Christian worship, and I gather one could find similar extremes in other traditions—for example, Reconstructionist services at one pole and Hasidic ecstasy at the other in Judaism.

Horizontally (noticing the participation of our own minds), Holmes notes the polar extremes of apophatic and kataphatic prayer that we have just discussed. Apophatic prayer is a kind of "emptying" (Transcendental Meditation is a form familiar to many Americans, though the TM people do not identify their technique as prayer), and kataphatic prayer is image-filled prayer of the kind exemplified by the psalms.

Summary

I urge that mental health professionals take more seriously the role of organized religion as a receptacle and organizer of core beliefs. Though we can be concerned about harmful cults masquerading as religion, we know that all religions began as "cults" and therefore, within reason, we may be well advised to suspend judgment, especially because evaluation of religion is particularly prone to projection and stereotyping. Such aspects of worship as prayer, ritual, metaphor, and authority need to be included in evaluations of organized religion, and different patterns of spirituality need to be acknowledged.

Religions are the oldest form of institutional organization that we know of. The major religions predate all known governments, psychologies, philosophies, and histories. They have provided safe havens and schools and cultural repositories second to none. They have connected our finite lives with the infinite. We have no evidence we can do without them.

Chapter Thirteen

Religious Worlds to Live In

It is the specific purpose of this chapter to review the context in which religious people live out their core beliefs. We have discussed the fact that core beliefs are personal, often unconscious, and frequently nonreligious in a conventional sense, but that most of the time they are lived out in a more or less deliberate institutional setting.

In addition to being not particularly prescient in understanding the evolution, persistence, and importance of the formal religious community in this country and elsewhere, social scientists, including mental health professionals like ourselves, are surprisingly uninformed about the ways in which institutional religion is organized. Under the best of circumstances, all of us, professional and lay alike, tend to be only vaguely aware of religious or even secular institutions that are not reflective of our own beliefs. But for more than half the population of the United States, living out belief systems involves a particular church, synagogue, or temple, and up to 90 percent of Americans profess a belief in God. However, it is my informal guess that the numbers would be much lower among mental health professionals, and this puts us at odds with many of our clients. This is especially unfortunate when church activities are central to a client's life. How are therapists to know when interview material is crucial, or even what questions to pursue, if they have no concept of the religious organization to which the client belongs?

This ignorance leads us into odd prejudices. Some years ago, when a friend invited me to attend a local Lutheran church with her, I was reluctant to go, afraid that I would be embarrassed by an old-fashioned sermon filled with dogmatic references to sin and embellished with none-too-subtle anti-Semitic references reflecting the church's origins in the ethnic German community in our town. I had a mental image of Lutherans as rigid and authoritarian in their beliefs. So I was happily surprised when the sermon turned out to be acceptably attuned to my personal biases, and the congregation (predominantly, though not entirely, white) friendly, interested in my point of view, and culturally varied.

When I finally talked with the pastor, my first hesitant question was, "Who *are* the Lutherans?" I told him that I had heard references to "synods" and known Lutherans elsewhere who did not believe in evolution and could not join the Boy Scouts because they were forbidden to take oaths, but that didn't seem to apply to the Lutherans in this church. His answer was that there are a number of separate Lutheran groups, referred to as "synods" among Lutherans, only loosely affiliated with one another and primarily sharing the basic teachings of Martin Luther. This led me to the discovery that most religious faiths in this country—Jewish, Buddhist, and Muslim, as well as Christian—are divided into subgroups or separate denominations that may have as many differences as commonalities.

I need to indulge in a little sociology of religion here, because I am convinced that basic information about how we are religiously organized is potentially useful to all of us in our encounters with clients. First of all, as previously mentioned and as I suppose we are all dimly aware, denominationalism turns out to be a main characteristic of religion in the United States; our religions, whatever their labels, come in many theological patterns largely because of their origins in different foreign lands. This has led to the establishment of ethnic churches under the aegis of all the major religions; it is as true of Judaism and Islam as of Christianity. J. Gordon Melton (1988) points out that a majority of religions have arrived here from elsewhere as expressions of national origins. When we speak of "Methodists" or "Baptists" or "Jews" or even "Muslims," as though this described some uniform group, we are betraying our ignorance.

This ethnic diversity has led to a second characteristic of American religions: with the exception of Judaism, they have always aggressively proselytized, trying to enlarge themselves and achieve dominance. Evangelicalism is so entrenched in the American character that we do not consider it peculiar to ourselves; because of the doctrine of church-state separation, our churches have not been dependent on government accreditation and support and have therefore been free to try to convert others and to theologize and reorganize to their hearts' content. The outcome of all this religious fervor is that we are collectively one of the most religious peoples on earth, and Melton notes that we have become not more ecumenical, as enthusiasts for church unity had predicted, but less so. At the end of the twentieth century, we are more varied than ever and have more denominations than ever, despite mergers in some of the mainline churches. Melton observes that this variety has had the serendipitous effect of preventing even the most aggressive denominations from dominating our political life, in spite of recent efforts of the conservative branches of the Christian churches to do so. The sole exception would be the influence of the Mormons in the state of Utah, but that is a very special case.

One caveat seems important to note. Churches tend to repackage themselves on a surprisingly regular basis: my reading suggests that any given denomination has a life span of twenty to forty years. Church politics are like secular politics: if the collective belief system strays too far from that of a large enough group of members, the group will split off and form a new church. This is presently happening in the Anglican-based churches, where the ordination of women and the adoption of a new prayer book have alienated many members; in the Southern Baptist Church, where fundamentalist members have taken control; and even in the Catholic Church, where abandonment of the Latin Mass on the one hand and a shortage of priests on the other have caused groups both right and left to set up irregular worship services in defiance of the church hierarchy. Even the relatively new American Buddhist community forms new centers and temples continuously. So anyone exploring a given church at a particular time needs to beware of assuming that what was true a decade ago still applies.

Nowhere can the problems and opportunities of what I am calling diversity be seen more clearly than in the multiplicity of beliefs, styles, organizations, and cultures of the various American Christian churches. The disadvantages and advantages of diversity are the same whether we are speaking of anthropological or religious systems, the obvious disadvantage being the continuous and sometimes bloody boundary disputes that have occurred over the years and the advantage being the constant renewal and vigor brought about by competition between churches.

Any institutional religion is ultimately the collective expression of individual core beliefs, the organized expression of personal convictions that both come from experience and lead to experience. So changing life experiences cause religions to remain somewhat fluid—a point worth remembering when trying to freeze religious systems in place with descriptive words such as these. Religions are both sociological, in that they grow out of the cultures in which they find themselves, and personal, in that they reflect their members' deepest conceptions of reality; in a sense, any church faces in two directions at once—inward toward its members' preferences and outward toward both the larger society within which it must exist and the ecclesiastical authority whom it must please.

In addition, religious beliefs and practices may tend to be developmental, as Kenneth Stokes (1982) and others have pointed out, changing from the concrete and literal beliefs of childhood to the ethical and more abstract concepts of which adults are capable. I am resisting including a more complete discussion of the developmental theories of religious experience here because I have some doubts about their validity; while I think it may sometimes be true that religious experience changes in the ways that Kenneth Stokes, James Fowler, and others have suggested, it is my own sense that religion responds to life experience in more complicated and idiosyncratic directions than a strictly developmental model would suggest. But whether these theories are true or not, any church must accommodate a great variety of conceptual modes and levels of maturity, and this provides an additional variable in determining its stability.

World religions are like large countries in that no single

description applies to the diverse beliefs and practices of their pop-
ulations. For example, just as we could not describe a universal attitude toward women, minorities, or labor unions in the United
States, so we cannot generalize about such attitudes in the world
religions. To some extent they reflect the countries in which they
exist; for instance, Roman Catholicism in the United States tends
to be more democratic than it is in many other parts of the world.
Islam has a more severe face in Saudi Arabia than in Egypt. European Lutherans find their American counterparts unnecessarily
intimate and collegial.

Again, we need to beware of stereotypes. Let us use women's
rights as an illustration. Professional Muslim women in the United
States are understandably defensive about the stereotype of subju-
gated Islamic women shrouded in veils whom we often see on our
TV screens. Reconstructionist Jews do not practice the same sort
of segregation of the sexes that is required by Orthodox Jews. Christians in general are as divided as the rest of Americans on the questions of abortion and women's rights.

To some extent these divisions reflect the different authority
traditions in any particular denomination or religion. To the extent
that the branch or denomination or particular teacher "leans into"
and tries to accommodate the culture within which the religion
exists (Reform Jews, mainline Protestants, some popular Buddhist
centers), beliefs and practices will tend to reflect that culture and
there will be a "loose" interpretation of scripture and tradition. By
contrast, where there is a hierarchical authority structure commit-
ted to preservation of doctrinal purity, as in some parts of the Muslim world, in Roman Catholicism, or in the "quasi-catholicism" of
the Lutheran and Anglican communities, scripture and tradition
may conflict with popular culture in such areas as women's rights,
sexual practices, and family law.

Organized religious communities in this country are far more
complicated than occasional attendance at church services might
suggest. Their parochial schools are probably the most visible ancil-
lary service of organized religions in the United States and represent most of the major denominations and religions, especially if

we include colleges and universities. Another supplementary educational activity that has had a powerful influence on many people is the operation of summer camps by nearly every denomination and major religion. I have had occasion to ask some young adults about their most memorable religious experience and have been surprised by how frequently they report experiences that occurred at church camps.

While on the subject of educational institutions, I would like to say a word here about seminaries, as even the word is unfamiliar to most people in the secular world. Seminaries are institutions of higher education whose major role is to educate professional clergy. Some of them are affiliated with traditional universities (Yale, Harvard, Princeton, Columbia, and Chicago are the most prominent ones), but most are freestanding colleges. Nearly every denomination supports at least one seminary and usually several. These days most seminaries offer graduate degrees: in the Christian churches, a Master of Divinity degree requires a three- or four-year graduate education, usually including some sort of internship in an institutional setting—church, hospital, counseling center, or community service center—and is the entry-level degree for ordination (designation as a member of the official clergy). Seminaries generally offer doctorates of several kinds. (Many African-American denominations and some fundamentalist churches ordain ministers after an apprenticeship in the church itself rather than after a seminary education.)

In addition to their educational endeavors, most major religious institutions support retreat centers of various kinds; within the Catholic community, convents and monasteries that would otherwise have to be abandoned because of declining membership within the orders have been reoriented as retreat centers, often administered by the nuns and monks of the order. Several Buddhist orders also have bought large old estates along the Hudson River and elsewhere and have turned them into retreat centers. These centers are available not only to members of the religion but often to the general public, and my experience with several of them is that they are gentle, nonintrusive, and respectful of traditions other than their own—wonderful resources for contemplation and escape from the stress of everyday life. (And the food can be surprisingly good, too!)

In the world at large, the charitable activities of the major religions are too often overlooked by the secular world. We may know about the American Friends Service Committee, which won the Nobel Peace Prize soon after the Second World War, but less well known are the service organizations of the Catholic, Lutheran, Jewish, Presbyterian, and other religions, which are major contributors to relief efforts throughout the world.

One other characteristic of American Christian churches in particular should be mentioned. In this country there exist a large number of unaffiliated, nondenominational churches, often calling themselves community churches, some of them of considerable size—in fact, several of the most populous churches in America are nonaffiliated. These churches are often associated with a famous pastor or are disenchanted offshoots of a conventional denomination. Because of their magnitude and independence, they may be appealing to persons who have had unhappy experiences with the mainline churches.

Whatever one's personal belief system, there is some form of organized religion to support it. Whatever one's psychological preferences, there are worship or meditation practices that should be congenial. As mental health professionals we owe it to our clients to understand and be familiar with the multiple ways in which the religious instinct expresses itself in their lives. No one need be alone in the universe; to some extent the universe expresses itself in those ancient and complex communities of otherworldly presence and metaphysical conviction that are the world's religions.

Chapter Fourteen

~

Religion and Mental Illness

In Chapter Fifteen I will discuss new approaches to mental health practice, but first I want to introduce the subject of mental illness. You must have wondered how the distortions of reality that we call mental illness fit into the premises of this presentation. Is it possible to make distinctions between normal, integrative belief systems and psychotic delusions? Can revelation be separated from schizophrenia? Though this is too broad a topic to treat at any length, I would like to address it briefly because it is widely recognized that the delusional systems of mentally ill persons may include religious ideas.

"Mental illness" is a concept that has scared professionals into discounting anomalous behavior or experience to such an extent that possible encounters with God have been compartmentalized into a category including all voices and visions of whatever origin or outcome. Such professional timidity has prevented our supporting and encouraging experiences of the transcendental, which can enrich and enlarge spiritual visions and provide spiritual maps for journeys through life's perilous and challenging landscape. Because legitimate religious experience itself often seems "crazy," professionals are understandably cautious in their assessments, but I am convinced that it is possible to sort out healthy transcendental experience from psychotic thought processes and to offer alternative possibilities for spiritual and psychological growth from those offered by psychiatric and medical intervention.

Note: Most of this material originally appeared as an article, "Awake in a Sea of Dreams," *Haelan* (Detroit: Ecumenical Theological Center, 1988).

How can we assess whether someone is having a genuine revelational experience or is exhibiting symptoms of psychosis? First,
by ruling out all of the ordinary criteria for mental illness, such as
unexplained changes in emotional state, so-called schizophrenic
affect (flatness, inappropriateness, incoherence), prolonged depression, and wide mood swings; these are widely understood and
accepted. From the reports of persons I have known who have had
inexplicable religious experiences, the crucial variable in whether
or not they will share the experience is whether the professional
listens with respect and does not insist on interpreting or otherwise
discounting the experience. There is certainly an almost unavoidable urge to explain away mystery, but if the listener begins to discern meaning and coherence, then I think we are safe in assuming
that something other than mental illness is involved.

Mental illnesses, as we will discuss them here, have tradition-
ally been considered to be of three distinctive varieties: the affective disorders (primarily unipolar and bipolar depression), the
behavioral disorders (sometimes called psychopathology or
sociopathology), and the cognitive disorders, especially the schizophrenias. Because they so often have religious components and
can be confused with conversion experiences and revelations, it is
the schizophrenias I want to address in this chapter.

Gerald May notes that even though schizophrenic episodes
resemble unitive ones in their distorted sense of time and blurred
sense of self, in many ways they are different. He describes the differences between unitive experiences (what I call "revelational
experience") and psychosis in an excellent section of *Will and Spirit*
(1982) titled "Unity and Insanity." (This book contains the best
explanation of the subject that I have encountered, and I recommend it to readers who would like a more exhaustive consideration.) The following is a part of what May says:

> In schizophrenia many changes occur in self-image, with
> marked distortions of body sense, strong ambivalences of desire and
> will, and deeply disturbed feelings of relationship. Changes in aware-

ness occur as well, with people sometimes reporting that their awareness became unusually bright and clear prior to a schizophrenic decompensation. Since self-image is so clearly affected in both schizophrenia and unitive experience, some psychiatrists have come to believe that all unitive experiences are pathological. The most common assumption is that such experiences represent a form of dissociation, a psychological defense mechanism in which certain contents are split off from awareness, resulting in an altered state of consciousness similar to hypnosis or some forms of amnesia. But several factors cast doubt upon this assumption. First, spontaneous unitive experiences occur frequently in the absence of identifiable stress or psychopathology. Second, the effects of unitive experience often seem to be highly integrative and creative, even despite the rebellion of self-image. Regardless of some recent psychiatric theories, I have never seen nor heard of a schizophrenic illness that either I or the patient could in any way identify as integrative, no matter how it was treated. Finally, it is often impossible to discern any psychodynamic or situational reason why unitive experiences occur when they do. They do not seem to be attempts to handle any special kind of anxiety or stress, nor do they usually seem to meet any special need other than the spiritual longing we have described [pp. 120–121].

Research suggests that true schizophrenia (assuming that there is such a generic category) is a physiological disorder affecting cognition, often showing its symptoms in early childhood and usually manifesting overt mental disorder in young adulthood. Some schizoid children fail to become adult schizophrenics and are merely odd adults—we all know them. Some become criminals or manifest their thought disorders in other kinds of antisocial behavior. There seems to be a schizophrenic continuum, with "ambulatory schizophrenics" managing routine tasks and driving their friends and relatives wild with their disordered logic, and "decompensated schizophrenics" sleeping (these days) on our park benches. But schizophrenics have a certain aura, and many psychiatrists have noted an inexplicable sense of the disorder. This sense is not a very helpful diagnostic tool, but I myself would use it in making clinical judgments.

I think of a lawyer's wife, Mrs. C.—beautiful, charming, odd—who came to me for counseling some years ago. After a few sessions, my sensors were on alert. I had trouble following her train of thought; A didn't seem to lead to B in her world. I asked her for a release of information and talked with a previous therapist. "Paranoid schizophrenic," said this weary old pro. "She'll drive you crazy." I was not sure I agreed with that diagnosis—I thought the therapist was overly exasperated with Mrs. C.—but she did seem to be driving her husband and children crazy, though *she* was not crazy in any ordinary sense of the word.

Was she likely to become openly psychotic—out of touch with reality? It is hard to say. The last I heard of her, she was divorced (her husband finally gave up), and no doubt she has had a succession of men in her life. I would lay odds that she was never married again for any length of time, that she probably developed a substance abuse problem, and that she will eventually show up in some geriatric clinic as a difficult and eccentric old woman whose children are, according to her, excessively mean to her—won't take care of her, won't let her live with them. I have a hunch that the wires in her mental circuitry were crossed from the start. Her entire life was a not entirely unsuccessful effort to cope with the strange mental states this neurological or chemical malfunction created for her.

Mrs. C. constructed rigid thought patterns that did not correspond to those of most people but that helped keep her mind under some semblance of control. Indeed, one of the red flags of her condition was the inflexibility of her thinking. She could not afford to experiment with mental shades of gray, which would leave her feeling as though her thoughts were straying into chaos. When stressed beyond a certain point, she became panicky and borrowed the ego strength and common sense of everyone around her—especially of the therapists she contacted from time to time. But however disorganized her personal life became, she managed to hang on to the real world by a slender thread.

Mrs. C. was a regular churchgoer but had no understanding of religious concepts. Abstractions of any kind were far too scary for her to deal with, and her poor minister was drawn into serving as another in her succession of therapists. The same rigid thought structure that kept her slightly sane could not handle the ambiguities of conventional religious beliefs. Had she decompensated, she might well have been flooded with strange religious ideas, or she might have joined a cult and thereby discovered, in doctrinaire rules, a new way to bring order to her disordered thoughts.

What of people who slip into psychotic episodes? Are they, by definition, schizophrenic? I used to play a simple game with my social work students. After defining *crazy* as "out of touch with reality," I asked them to write down a description of a time when they thought they were crazy. I then asked for a show of hands of those who could think of such a time. Invariably, more than half the students would raise their hands. (I never asked students to share what they wrote down, though I admit to curiosity. I was merely trying to make the point that occasional slippages are common and normal.) I am not convinced that occasional craziness is diagnostic of anything but stress; given enough stress, nearly everyone will eventually become "crazy"—our stress tolerances vary. But this is not schizophrenia. It is simply how our individual minds, with their differing capacities to organize stimuli, protect themselves from emotional and cognitive overload.

In one of my cases illustrating a stress-related psychosis, religion itself was a variable. Wilma, age thirty-five, had become interested in a charismatic religious group and began attending their services. She had never before had any religious affiliation, but she had grown up in a succession of foster homes and welcomed the "family feeling" of her new church. She had earned a college degree, was married to an emotionally disorganized but otherwise sane husband, and was the mother of an attractive child whom I knew slightly. At the time of her psychotic episode, she had lost nearly fifty pounds and was hardly recognizable. She had begun an affair with her boss—a first for her, as her fat self had not been attractive to men.

One day she appeared in my office high as a kite. Her thinking was filled with religious paranoia. Talking nonstop, she told me how dreadful the religious group was and how they had ruined her life. She went on and on, and before I could say much in response, she abruptly stood up and left. Later that night, her husband had her admitted to the state hospital. She was diagnosed with a "character disorder" (a commentary on state hospitals of that era) and was released the next day.

Did the charismatic religion push her off the tracks? I would torment myself with that question—after all, I had encouraged the affiliation and defended the group to her husband, a nominal member of a mainline Protestant denomination. The evening of her breakdown, it was tempting to blame religion for her troubles, but in retrospect I have come to think that Wilma simply snapped under too much stress: too many diet pills, too much illicit romance, too much success in her job (she had recently been promoted), and too much overheated optimism in her new religion. She had a fragile emotional heritage that may have made her susceptible to cognitive and emotional flooding, and for the first and as far as I know the only time in her life, she was overwhelmed.

Some time later, Wilma used me as a reference in her custody fight, and my first question to the court worker was, "Is she chubby?" I was reassured to learn that she was. The slim Wilma made me uneasy; she needed those familiar physical boundaries. She had married her boss, had quit her job, and was no longer riding on the organized optimism of charismatic Christianity or defending herself against their moral strictures.

Had I to do it over, would I discourage Wilma's involvement with what had been referred to in some circles as a "holiness sect"? It immediately occurs to me that it was not up to me to decide. My prior experience with this group had been positive; two clients and one social acquaintance who were members seemed to derive benefits from membership. It would have been dishonest not to acknowledge this personal mind-set, at least to myself. Had Wilma's husband participated with her, I think the outcome might have been different; there probably would have been no affair, and the support of the group for the marriage would have balanced its rigid rules. Wilma was a sensitive and emotional person. She had functioned at a high level for most of her adult life and had been able to integrate many new ideas without losing emotional equilibrium. (Interestingly, this charismatic group no longer accepts half of a married couple; they recognize that this may foment family dissension.)

What of chronic schizophrenics with religious delusions (common thought disorders found in any psychiatric population)? How does religion fit into a discussion of someone like this? Why do schizophrenics sometimes fall off the edge and think they are Christ? Do the illusions of being Christ cause the schizophrenia, or does the schizophrenia cause the illusions? When schizoid persons encounter an illusory system of ideas, does such a system cause them to decompensate? I contend that religious systems in themselves are not the cause of psychosis but rather furnish content for the disordered thinking.

I once worked with a woman I will call Bridget. She was referred by a pastor who was puzzled and impressed by what he called "her visions." She had seen the Virgin Mary and had been having experiences with what she alleged were "demonic influences." When I asked what the meaning content of these visions and experiences was, the pastor seemed unsure. She had talked with several priests who seemed impressed with her, and one had even tried to exorcise the demons. The pastor knew nothing of her background but was aware that she was extremely frightened by what was happening to her. She was beginning to have physical symptoms, a sense of something evil invading her body and crawling up her arms and legs. The pastor had heard that I had worked with people who were having spiritual experiences and wondered if I had anything to suggest.

Why was I sure, even before I talked with her, that Bridget was a decompensating schizophrenic? For one thing, her visions seemed to have no coherent content. They were frightening impressions and nightmarish anomalies, but in no sense were they uplifting or unified or healing. Furthermore, the physical manifestations were characteristic of a schizophrenic breakdown. From every angle, the impression was of disintegration. Religious experts speak of "edification" in describing religious ecstasy. Neither Bridget nor any of the people with whom she had talked were edified by her experiences; quite the contrary, everyone seemed to be thoroughly alarmed. (My unscientific observation is that when I feel alarmed or irritated or confused by someone who does not seem to be doing anything overt to cause those reactions, I am alerted to the possibility of mental illness.)

The moment I talked with Bridget on the phone, I knew that my suspicions were correct. Her voice was flat and without normal intonation; she spoke in a kind of whining monotone. Later, when I saw her for the first time, I was struck by her very bright and unblinking eyes, though she was in other ways attractive, carefully groomed, and socially appropriate. She accepted my explanation that she was physically ill and needed to see a doctor immediately. Indeed, she seemed greatly relieved by this information. Within twenty-four hours, she was on one of the antipsychotic drugs and was feeling somewhat better, but her psychiatrist explained that he was afraid to start her on a large dose, so within two weeks her symptoms returned and she eagerly and desperately drove herself to the hospital and admitted herself to an open psychiatric unit. When I talked with her on the phone about a week later, the "evil forces" had left her body, and she was planning a weekend leave. She was to need ongoing psychiatric support to enable her to adjust to her environment and to understand her illness, but the visions seemed to have been cured by medication.

Bridget was extremely anxious for her delusions to be accepted as "real," and we can strain our minds considering the implications of the word *real* in this case. I assume she meant that she didn't want us to think she was imagining what was happening, that it was solely the product of her disordered mind. Because her abstract reasoning was the lightning rod down which the delusions traveled, there was no possibility of discussing existential realities with her; we would then only add to her already unmanageable input of ideas.

But when I consider what I think the realities were, I am returned to my conviction that in some odd way the mind ordinarily acts as a prism, organizing a universe of stimuli and meaning that we refract into individual and unique creations of individual consciousness. Mental illness is, by definition, a condition that either blocks out larger meaning or allows it to flood in on itself through "somatizing" (diverting thoughts into physical symptoms, such as Bridget's feelings in her arms and legs, and into sensory delusions) and through desperately assigning meaning to the influx of chaotic ideas, using whatever existential paradigm is available, often from the world of religious concepts, which offers our only lexicon and topography for metaphysical quests.

In the case of Wilma, the additional burden of emotional ideas from her new religion, her sexual adventures, and the change in her physical condition caused a similar flooding of her cognitive processes—a brief psychotic episode. Mrs. C. protected herself from psychosis by keeping inflexible boundaries around her thoughts, though in many ways her problem was the most serious. If the schizophrenic outcome is caused by a physiological flaw in the mind's ability to process data, it does not matter what the origin of the thought disorder may be, whether some chemical malfunction (including a nutritional deficit, as has been postulated in some quarters), some genetic flaw, or some overwhelming trauma. Ultimately, the only helpful treatment of schizophrenia seems to be simplification of external stimuli (to the point that the individual can handle the sensory input) and chemical intervention to improve the processing ability of the brain.

In the past, some therapists (and for opposite reasons, some pastors) have become so preoccupied with the symptoms—the delusional ideas—that they have virtually ignored the physical illness. But if we accept the hypothesis that schizophrenia is a thought disorder with a variety of probable causes, in which the mind loses its ability to screen and organize sensory input, then the crucial consideration is not the content of the psychotic thoughts but rather the disordered process itself, and not only is protecting ourselves from internal images and waking dream states unnecessary for well people, but such overprotectiveness also cruelly impoverishes our spiritual experience. Distinguishing appropriate states of wellness then becomes the task of the inner healer in each of us, a task that we are usually able to accomplish. The gatekeeping of transcendental experience does not seem to me to be an appropriate one for mental health professionals, who might more usefully explore the emotional and intellectual enrichment that transcendental experience often provides for their clients.

It can hardly be overemphasized that acute mental illness is frightening to the sufferer. A loving and supportive therapist or pastor can facilitate contact with a physician or psychiatrist, and it is at best irresponsible and at worst cruel not to be aware of such illnesses when they appear in one's office. But the bottom-line question is, Can revelational experiences be distinguished from psychotic illusions? The answer is, Of course they can; they are polar opposites. Revelational experiences are unifying, edifying, love-producing, growth-enhancing, and experienced with interest and joy. Psychoses are disintegrative, self-destructive, frightening, inconsistent, and usually experienced as aversive and confusing. The only commonality seems to be their origin in the unconscious, and in the case of schizophrenia, even that assumption is probably not correct, because there seems to be strong evidence that it is a physical illness. If counselors and therapists will listen carefully to what individuals have to report about their experiences, a helpful stance will emerge—medical referral for the mentally ill person and supportive reassurance for the mystic.

Chapter Fifteen

———

Spirituality and Therapeutic Practice

"We try to help them express their unexpressed, in some cases even unrecognized, emotions before they cease to exist," the therapist explained to students in his counseling class. Before the patients cease to exist, he meant, referring to terminally ill cancer patients who were participating in a group he had organized and led. The video camera then showed us a session of that group, seven or eight patients with metastatic cancer, carefully, painfully revealing to one another (and to us) what that awful reality meant to them. The patients seemed oblivious to the intrusive presence of the camera as they talked about how it felt to have cancer, how they were managing to cope, how life had changed for them. We then saw several more partial sessions taking place weeks later. We learned that the members had begun socializing with one another outside the group, that one man had died, and that they had become a genuine emotional support system for one another. But the word God was never spoken during the course of the segments we saw. No one ever asked the really big question: What do you think happens after you die?

However, I thought to myself, when the patients were having coffee together after the formal sessions were over, surely that question came up, surely it was on everyone's minds. To this viewer at least, it seemed clear that the therapist's assumption that death is the "end of human existence," as he candidly put it to the class (not, I presume, to the group), created an unspoken limit to what the group members felt permission to talk about during the formal meetings—their feelings, their families, their pain, but not their futures in this world or the next. The way the group operated struck me as archaic, out of another time, a smugly secular approach to therapy. I was reminded of how different that approach was from the attitude toward the dying I experienced when I was consultant to a hospice agency in the late 1980s. In that organization we routinely had a member of the clergy available for both case conferences and individual patient support, and it was assumed that dying patients always would be invited to share their spiritual and religious beliefs—practices, disappointments, questions—if they wished to do so. If necessary, we would scout out religious resources for individuals who had not previously had any available to them.

I once led therapy groups that resembled the videotaped one I just described. But gradually over the years, the knot in my stomach over the unspoken restrictions on what was "politically correct" therapy caused me to strike out on my own, eventually to leave teaching and the agency for which I worked. The realization that religion and spirituality could be incorporated into a counseling practice took longer to evolve and was related to the Doctor of Ministry program in which I eventually enrolled out of my eagerness to study theology and my curiosity about the world of organized religion.

When I began the project from which this book derives, nearly twenty years ago at this writing, the mental health profession was just beginning to shake off the chains of what many of us would agree was a too-rigid scientific orthodoxy. In graduate school in the 1960s, we were still arguing about psychoanalysis versus behaviorism, as if those were the only therapeutic choices, and even ego psychology was considered a slightly radical departure from conventional wisdom. When in 1975 I cautiously ventured out to California from my home in Michigan to spend a month studying Gestalt therapy (which no one I knew had heard of), I wondered what kind of nuttiness I was getting into and was warned by colleagues and friends to protect myself from therapeutic cults and grandstanding gurus. It is hard to realize that such a relatively short time ago, alternative therapies, including group therapy, were suspect—too threatening to fragile egos, too confrontational, too unconfidential. Transpersonal psychology did not exist, and humanistic psychology was in an embryonic state. Furthermore, except for Victor Frankl (1992 [1959]), I did not know of any social scientists who were including considerations of the spiritual in their writing. There was a sense of bootlegging, of illegitimacy, to any religious or spiritual conversations held with colleagues or clients.

I recall an adoption study I once conducted in which the husband had been converted to Christianity at a Billy Graham rally. In every way I was convinced that the couple would be exemplary parents, but I omitted information about the religious conversion from my report because I was sure it would prejudice the adoption supervisor against them. Yet in a 1993 bulletin, the University of Michigan School of Social Work advertised two courses in spirituality. One was called Social Work and Spirituality; the other, Creativity and Clinical Practice: The Inner Journey and the Outward Dance. The descriptions referred to "the wisdom of spiritual traditions"; promised guided meditation, journaling, and dreamwork exercises; and asked, "How do we tap into and encourage creative expression in the lives of our clients and ourselves?" We have come a long way. Today the word *spiritual* seems to be on everyone's lips, though I sense that many professionals do not quite make the connection between *spiritual* and *religious*, religion still being suspect in many psychological quarters. But the realization that we are spiritual beings no longer seems fanciful.

As we discussed earlier, organized religion itself reflects this reawakening of the spiritual in the renewal movements of the late twentieth century; around the earth, religions are returning to their other-worldly origins. Ira Progoff (1980) explains this by pointing out that religions continuously renew themselves by returning to their inner sources through meditation and prayer; that to the extent they become too worldly, too "outer," they lose vitality. As he nicely puts it, "If they have only the external, their contact with the sources of spiritual experience dries up and there is no inspiration for periodic renewal" (p. 27). We have begun to realize that the same comment can be made about psychology. Progoff's own efforts to return people to their inner resources through intensive journaling is one of the techniques we will examine shortly.

Critics have complained that the return to earlier belief systems, which accept mystery as more than just ignorance and worship as more than just credulousness, is merely a retreat in the face of presumably temporary obstacles that will sooner or later be overcome. But I am proposing here that we are in the middle of a revolution in the fields of counseling and psychotherapy. As people have resisted having their spiritual beliefs discounted by science, so too a strictly scientific approach to psychology—an approach wedded to evidence and controls and experiment—has been diluted by the rediscovery of creativity, imagination, and reverence. The freedom that the loosening of scientific absolutism has allowed means that psychology no longer is required to exclude religious beliefs because they are "outside of science" and that experiments in alternative psychologies have been able to enter the mainstream of therapeutic possibility without embarrassment or apology.

However, problems remain. The fact that modern technology causes changes to occur at lightning speed does not help us in sorting out the efficacious from the merely popular, whether we are speaking of new therapies or new religions. It is fascinating to question whether belief systems, both psychological and religious, change with the same rapidity as technology. We are witnessing a proliferation of odd alternative cults in psychology as well as religion; it remains to be seen if this represents only prurient interest and public sensationalism or whether new therapies of lasting impact are emerging. One sometimes has a sense of the confusion of individuals without well-integrated beliefs who are thrown to the wolves of television docudramas and talk shows.

And residues of old attitudes remain. Not long ago, I attended a social work conference and ran into a former professor of mine. He was curious about my current activities, so I told him about my religious pilgrimage and my studies. "What are you going to do next?" he asked me with what I am sure was genuine interest. "I'll wait to see where I am led," I replied. His face went blank. It was as if I had poured a glass of cold, irrational water on what had been a promising conversation. He finally responded, "That strikes me as a rather reactive position," and then our conversation stopped. It was clear that he could not think how to proceed.

The concept of "leadings"—the idea that one is "intended" to proceed in a particular way—seems to be a sticking point. (In this I am reminded of Ernest Becker's wise advice to remain open and wait.) It is the place where I can imagine some former colleagues putting down this book in bewilderment, as if all their carefully learned techniques of assessment and intervention were about to be pitched out of a fanatic's window. Perhaps they forget that they themselves attend to "unconscious material" to clarify their own or their clients' reasons for life choices or to puzzle over dreams during watershed times in life—after all, many conclusions are reached and decisions made for reasons not so rational as might appear on the surface. So whether the leading comes out of one's own personal unconscious or whether it is related, in the Jungian sense, to the Self—the collective unconscious—or more elusively to the synchronicities that present themselves in our lives (or whether, in religious terms, it comes from God), paying attention to deep inner messages seems to many of us to be a sound methodology. In fact, when our choices do not acknowledge our inner voices, we may find ourselves on roads reflecting neither our talents nor our unique individualities—inauthentic, unproductive, uninspiring.

I would like in this chapter to sketch ways in which religion and psychology have melded in a number of therapeutic approaches. In trying to devise an outline for these approaches, I struggled with the realization that they tend to have short "half lives." But in spite of the pace with which one method evolves into another—and this is what I think happens; I do not believe that methods become wholly obsolete—there are certain commonalities that allow us to make a generalized survey, much as we were able to do with religious organizations.

Reviewing the therapies and projects with which I am familiar, I observe they can be divided into general categories, each of which contains elements of both traditional psychology and what we are calling "spirituality"—the creative, mystical, and numinous. I will try to show how each of these categories applies to direct practice, but once again I remind you that mental health practice is a very big arena, extending far beyond one-on-one or couples therapy in a traditional office setting. Mental health practice operates in institutions such as schools, hospitals, and prisons, "on the streets," in drug treatment centers, in community clinics, and in a wide variety of group treatment settings. So I ask you to open your imagination and consider whether some of the innovative approaches described in this chapter might be useful in these various settings. The techniques I am advocating include journaling, meditation, dialogues, groups, and retreat centers.

Journaling

Many adolescents—I was no exception—discover journaling all by themselves. That delicious little spiral notebook filled with one's most emotional secrets becomes a repository for thoughts and feelings that might cause an overload explosion without an escape valve such as writing. Furthermore, one can later relive one's own experiences by rereading what is written down and thus discover who one really is. As Morton Kelsey (1984, p. 131) puts it, "We become more of who we are when we express what we experience ourselves to be."

The same rationale applies to the journaling that is advocated for adults. Ira Progoff, Ignatius of Loyola, and Morton Kelsey are only three of a number of psychological and spiritual teachers who have realized that if individuals can write down their thoughts and feelings, these become available for analysis and change. And for the same reason that adolescents find writing to be a way of organizing thoughts and taming emotions, adults can use writing to examine their inner lives, including their dreams, prayers, intuitions, and feelings. Furthermore, when we have a journal available, we can record experiences as they occur—immediately upon wakening, for example, or after a time of prayer or meditation—while the thoughts and feelings are fresh and clear or, as Progoff puts it, fluid and in process.

Progoff is a depth psychologist, therapist, lecturer, and workshop leader who has spent more than twenty-five years developing what he calls a "process meditation" method of journaling, with explicit spiritual goals. After his experiences in World War II, he began wondering what would have happened to humanity if Hitler had succeeded in burning all the religious books in the world—all the holy scriptures. It occurred to Progoff that we would not, in fact, be bereft because the source of those scriptures would remain in the inner lives of holy people or perhaps even in the inner lives of ordinary people who took the time to search. "We would simply draw new spiritual scriptures from the same great source out of which the old ones came" (Progoff, 1980, p. 10). That being so, he then began to wonder why we do not plumb those spiritual depths even though our scriptures have *not* been destroyed. And he realized that our relationship to our own scriptures would be enhanced if we could connect them with our inner lives. In his words, "There are many modern persons who accept the validity of the ancient religious teachings even to the point of revering them, and yet do not have an effective way of relating them to the urgent and immediate needs of daily life" (p. 13).

Out of Progoff's studies of depth psychology and his search for underlying principles of religious creativity came his "Intensive Journal" workshops. Although the original goal was the discovery of inner spiritual resources, some unexpected serendipities evolved out of his new format. He found that participants were able to unlock resources within themselves for the understanding and integration of many of the "stuck" places in their lives and that the process seemed to generate energy and optimism. He hypothesized that "its nonanalytic approach generates a movement of inner energies" (Progoff, 1980, p. 16).

The Progoff journaling technique differs from other journaling methods in that it involves interrelated notebook sections or topical units that are designed to work together to produce entirely new "emergents," psychological and spiritual integrations that are not predictable on the basis of the individual's prior experiences or understandings. He explains, "Emergents come about as the great unexpected and unexplained leaps when something altogether new enters the world" (Progoff, 1980, p. 58), and he has found the structured journaling notebooks to be a way of recording and integrating the meditative process. He is concerned to keep inner experience as fluid as possible and is interested in the way units of life ebb and flow and merge over time. He says of this theory, "Working with the hypothesis of process enables us to draw together large amounts of subjective and intangible material while they are still in their living movement. . . . Conceiving life as a process, we can have a continuing relation with it. We can dialogue with it. We can evoke latent capacities contained within it, and we can help develop them. We can work together with our life as a process, reconsidering with it what it wishes to become, and helping it arrive at the place where together we decide it should go" (pp. 42–43).

A sort of process recording has been used for decades by students learning to be therapists, but a modification of the Progoff technique, a sort of diary keeping, can be used by individuals seeking to translate isolated life experiences into coherent units of meaning and significance, to develop a sense not only of self but also of connection to larger life purposes. By sharing journals with therapists or group members, recurrent themes (as well as obstacles) become clear, and a patterned "life story" begins to emerge. Many senior citizen centers are already using writing workshops, and intentional "life review" journals using topical headings are intervention possibilities for alert residents of some nursing homes as well. (Tape recorders can substitute for writing where appropriate.) You yourself may have asked clients to record dreams for use in therapy; I would like to suggest that "free-associating" on paper in connection with dream recordings is useful as well, giving the dream a title, for example, and continuing the plot to a satisfactory resolution. (I thank John Biersdorf for this technique.)

Related to Progoff journaling in the sense of keeping an ongoing record of life processes but with an explicitly spiritual emphasis is the journaling emerging from the Ignatian Exercises. Ignatius of Loyola, founder of the Jesuit order of the Roman Catholic Church, lived in sixteenth-century Spain. Out of his personal soul searching came a method of meditation, known as the Ignatian Exercises, that has been in use ever since. I had personal experience with this kind of meditation journaling during my own participation in the Ignatian Exercises. I would read a prescribed spiritual passage of some sort and then meditate with my eyes closed for thirty or forty minutes. This enabled the emergence into my quieted mind of mental images, messages, emotions, and "consolations" (a famous Ignatian concept) of peculiar power. I would then promptly write down whatever images or messages I seemed to have received. (I cannot identify their source with certainty, but sometimes they were unexpectedly vivid and surprising.) Both meditations and journal were intended to integrate spiritual and psychological experiences, and the discernment of the value of these experiences came from the guidance of the spiritual director (who, in my judgment, was a sort of therapist, though she often protested that characterization). For clients with an active prayer life, this method of journaling offers great potential, and I recommend that therapists wishing to pursue it seek out material on the Ignatian Exercises in the library or contact a Roman Catholic diocese for more information.

The last journaling advocate I want to mention is the priest, teacher, and writer Morton Kelsey, who has written many compelling books on the subjects of spirituality and psychology. One of his most original and useful contributions is a method of journaling using prayer and dialogue. His book *Adventure Inward* (1979a) provides an explicit methodology for keeping a personal journal, as well as an explanation for the effectiveness of this activity. Kelsey analyzes the power of a personal journal in the following ways: it helps us remember and gives continuity to life, it stimulates imagination, it helps us explore our emotional depths, it helps us remember and work with our dreams, it encourages personal growth, and it helps us evolve a personal relationship with God. He cautions, however, that as with any exploration of inner life, journaling can expose us to the dark places in our souls and should be undertaken only by persons who feel compelled to record their lives. Kelsey offers very specific methods for keeping a journal, and if I were counseling a religious person who wished to begin jour-naling, I would suggest Kelsey's books because they are clearly writ-ten, without any arcane concepts or language, and could be easily implemented.

In direct practice, I can envision mental health workers in institutional settings of all kinds encouraging people to record and share their feelings, prayers, and dreams in personal journals or diaries. I would answer critics who argue that this is not mental health practice that if it is not, it should be, because journaling can open up inner thoughts and feelings and keep clients in touch with their lives between sessions with group and therapist. Furthermore, journaling need not be in prose. If someone has poetic impulses, the journal can contain their poems, even their prayers. Or the journal can be a repository for quotations of various kinds or letters that need to be written but not mailed. And all of these entries can be shared with a group—that is, in fact, an excellent way to struc-ture a group session and to encourage participation—or with a ther-apist or a pastoral counselor, mental health resources all.

Meditation

As you may have observed, meditation is often a component of journaling, and it is also, of course, an integral aspect of prayer. Meditation techniques are taught in classical forms by Buddhist groups, by such popular organizations as Transcendental Medita-tion, as part of the Ignatian Exercises, by the Quakers as part of "unprogrammed worship," and by many healers both inside and outside the medical community (see Moyers, 1993). I want to sug-gest here that meditation is a wonderful adjunct to therapy, both within the counseling context and as a centering device in daily life.

Meditation can be thought of as a disciplined method of achieving altered states of consciousness, even a kind of self-hyp-nosis, though I realize regular practitioners will find that an overly simplistic explanation. However, it is often pointed out that each of us "meditates" several times every day; how often have you stood at a window, gazing at a snow-covered tree or a flower-filled garden, "lost in thought"? Were you not, at that moment, meditating? When you sit with your Bible, a book of poetry, or a love-filled letter from a friend and find your mind slipping away into reverie, are you not meditating? When you waken in the morning still half-engrossed in a dream and let your mind wander through the dream memory without censorship, is that not a form of meditation? Meditation is not an other-worldly, esoteric mystery; it is a familiar part of everyday life. But meditation comes in many packages. It can be learned and practiced as a method of purifying thought, in the Buddhist way, or it can be a way of exploring our rich subconscious imagery, as taught by Ignatius, Kelsey, Harold Edwards, and others. For many people, meditation has become a relaxing and illuminating technique for centering and freeing the mind from habitual patterns of activity and for loosening the imagination in the service of deeper understanding.

Content-filled meditations can be thought of as "waking dreams" and are extremely helpful in revealing to us our hidden, unconscious self. To some extent, the free-association technique of psychoanalytical therapy could be thought of as meditation, though I think there are some differences. My strong impression is that the content of my thoughts was very different when I was stringing together impressions and feelings and memories in a therapy session from when I was "watching" images and words appear in Ignatian contemplation. For one thing, the free association was value-neutral: whatever happened, happened. But in contemplation there was an underlying alertness, almost out of awareness, to images that appeared to be from God and those that appeared to be merely out of my own unconscious or, more ominously, seemed to contain evil. This is an odd danger that Gerald May (1982, p. 273) describes as "something very deep and subtle, exerting itself at the most primitive levels of energy differentiations, far beneath the realm of symbolism. It is neither horned nor serpentine, and it is nameless, but it can be perceived obviously, directly, and immediately as evil." It is this danger that accounts for the reluctance most people have to leave the world of commonsense thought, and

I wonder if it also accounts for the reluctance people often have to engage in therapy. "I don't want to know what's going on in there," they say, as if we all understand that there are dark forces that we would tune in to if we turned on our psychic transmitters. These fears are addressed by the presence of a spiritual director, whose task is the discernment of good and evil in the directee's life, or the presence of a therapist who creates a safe space within which the client can explore the content of his or her unconscious mind.

Another form of meditation that has become increasingly popular in recent years is called "guided imagery." In this meditative technique, espoused by Roberto Assagioli and others and introduced to me by the pastor and therapist Harold Edwards, clients are encouraged to close their eyes and relax, and then an image or an outline of a story is offered by the guide—a place such as a house, a meadow, or a temple—followed by a scenario such as a journey or an encounter with an ambiguous person or creature (there are a variety of standard scenarios). As the broad outline of the story unfolds, the clients give it their own images and provide details that enhance and enlarge it. It becomes a waking dream, but with a predetermined structure enabling the therapist or guide to direct the content of the dream to a certain extent.

This form of meditation is being used as a healing methodology in many places: as a means of spiritual exploration in religious settings, as a journey into the unconscious by Jungian analysts, and as a journey into the imagination in many different structured-group settings. I have frequently used it during counseling sessions to help a client pursue an image or thought that seems to recur but not go anywhere. I find that by simply asking the person to relax, close his or her eyes, let the image appear, and then see what it wants to do or where it wants to go—and allowing plenty of open, uninterrupted time—the individual's mind will often reveal the hidden meaning of whatever is going on.

There is great benefit in sharing content-filled meditations with other people: a therapist, other group members, a spiritual director, or a teacher such as a Buddhist priest. Religious people often share their meditations with God as a part of their prayer lives, and I suppose one reason that journaling is so often advocated as a part of meditation is that it also is a form of sharing. My own experience is that deep, unconscious imagery of whatever origin needs to find an outlet in words or other creative activity so as not to be merely returned to the unconscious in the same form. In my judgment, this is a primary reason for recording and analyzing dreams. (Content-free meditation such as TM or apophatic prayer has the effect of "washing the mind" and provides mind liberation of another kind.)

Mental health professionals trained in traditional methods are understandably wary of a technique as direct and obviously power-ful as guided imagery. My own experience is that this caution is unnecessary. Induced meditation in the therapeutic setting is not more esoteric than the sort of desensitization imagery used by behaviorists for decades and offers an opportunity for the imagina-tion to participate in the therapy in a vivid way. I have also found guided imagery to be a wonderful way to get clients "out of their heads" when too much rational analysis becomes an obstacle to progress. In terms of the theme of this book, the slightest permis-sion from the therapist can often release religious and spiritual imagery in clients for whom these are normative and comfortable and has the additional advantage of being less embarrassing than a head-on description.

For a wonderfully complete book of meditational and other spiritual exercises, I highly recommend Tilden Edwards's *Living in the Presence* (1987), which details specific methods of prayer and meditation without doctrinal rigidities (though Edwards's own ori-entation is Christian) and also offers a philosophy of spirituality that would be enlightening, I think, to mental health profession-als of many backgrounds.

Dialogues

I was first introduced to imaginary dialogues through the empty-chair technique of Fritz Perls when I was learning Gestalt therapy. As is well known by now, one "externalizes" an imagined person, object, thought, or emotion (I once dialogued with "sadness") by putting that projection in an empty chair and talking to it. One then "becomes" the projection by sitting in the formerly empty chair and speaking back to oneself, as if one *were* the sadness (or whatever). One moves back and forth between the two facing chairs, speaking first as one's conscious self and then as one's projection, until eventually the differences between projection and self begin to blur and dissolve. One has, at that point, "owned the projection," as the popular phrase puts it.

I recall a fellow workshop member asking what to do with a client who wanted to blame everything on God, and Erv Polster suggesting that God be placed in the empty chair. At first it seemed like an irreverent suggestion, but it soon became apparent that God was, for this person, as for most of us, a projection much like any other. So when I read Morton Kelsey's suggestion that dialogues with God become part of one's journaling activity, I was both suspicious and bemused. But because I remain convinced that our understanding of God is necessarily projective (we interpret the Divine Other on the basis of our background and experience), Kelsey's suggestion provides a powerful vehicle for examining our own intercourse with God (or whomever). However irrational the idea may seem, I have found when I have tried this that I have obtained surprising insight and even challenges from the voice that talked to me on paper. Whether that voice is, as seems probable, my own inner wisdom or whether it comes from somewhere else is perhaps irrelevant. (Kelsey spends a fair amount of time warning against "automatic writing"—the delusion that God has somehow taken control of the pen—and that does remain a hazard in trying this technique.)

The dialoguing technique has been effectively used in a number of nonreligious contemporary therapies, including transactional analysis and neurolinguistic programming (where ego parts can talk with each other) and psychosynthesis (where subpersonalities can have their say). Whenever a client's progress is blocked by an unowned projection or an unrecognized subpersonality, some sort of dialogue technique can be helpful.

Groups and Retreat Centers

Group therapies, ranging from Twelve-Step programs like Alcoholics Anonymous to the kinds of encounter groups used in drug treatment programs, are common knowledge. Unstructured support groups meet on topics ranging from cancer to the death of a child to separation and divorce. Churches, too, have begun to rely on similar groups, and consultants such as Charles Olsen (1984) and Gerald May (1979) offer careful and explicit suggestions for the formation of religious support groups. The Cursillo movement in the liturgical churches offers intensive group experiences leading to renewed commitment to social action. In the same way, the marriage encounter movement in the church community has proved to be a powerful mental health resource for religious people.

The power of the intentional small group remains as astonishing to me today as when I first organized one more than twenty years ago. I suppose no sea change in mental health treatment seems as hopeful as the acceptance of group therapy by the traditional mental health community.

I have alluded several times to intentional religious *communities*, and I would like to say more about them here. Though not groups in the technical sense, they are similar in that they promote mutual support between members and have common goals. As with groups, these are almost too numerous to list, but I have in mind such places as Pendle Hill; The Guild for Psychological Studies at Four Springs, California; religious retreat centers (as mentioned earlier, often operated by convents and monasteries); some special drug treatment centers; and any other refuges from conventional life in which there are opportunities for quiet reflection, personal growth, and worship. I think these are frequently overlooked by professionals who could easily use them as places of refuge for overwhelmed clients needing rest and a change of scenery more than anything else. Imagine how much more therapeutic a quiet, clean, supportive convent with nonintrusive sisters and good food would be than an institutional setting such as a hospital. The best way to locate such resources is to begin by calling the central offices of major churches, which can be identified through local clergy. Ask to talk with people who have visited the retreat center or other resource place, much as you would if trying to select a resort or a school. Or better yet, visit the place yourself! I call these places and people to the attention of all who are concerned with emotional and spiritual health as being potential allies and guides in our common quest. The fact that it rarely occurs to mental health professionals to use religious resources such as these as adjuncts to treatment has more to do with our ideological blind spots than with the quality of the resources. If I had a Roman Catholic client or a client for whom mystical experience seemed important, I would without hesitation advocate a guided retreat in a center that I had investigated and whose personnel I knew.

Summary

As interest in the spiritual dimension of mental health increases and new techniques and therapeutic philosophies become incorporated into conventional mental health practices, the old separation of religious and psychological concerns begins to seem old-fashioned and unnecessary. No longer do mental health clients have to sit in a chair in a professional office and answer questions or lie on a couch for months at a time and free-associate. Out of religious communities and the new psychologies have simultaneously evolved a number of innovative approaches to mental health, and these are suggesting new directions for practice with our expanding and diverse clientele. We have reviewed only a few of these here and note with hope (and no small amount of apprehension) that our explosive communications networks and shrinking world offer possibilities for many more.

Chapter Sixteen

Facing into the Future

The newspaper picture showed Russians in Moscow undergoing full-immersion baptism by the Jehovah's Witnesses. I had an immediate, intense feeling of pity for the Russians—poor victims, being taken advantage of like that! But when I read the accompanying article, it occurred to me that had the picture been of Russians in an Orthodox church, my reaction would have been very different: I would have been glad that the church was resurgent and that at last oppressed people were free to worship as they pleased. Later I realized that this was a vivid example of how prejudices rule emotions where religion is concerned. If I stepped back and thought about it rationally, I could see no reason why the Jehovah's Witnesses should not evangelize in Russia as elsewhere; using the criteria I myself have suggested, they have a time-tested tradition, they are true to Scripture as they read it, and their religion is "joyful and illuminating."

We have stressed that we all live as if certain realities are true, even though we have no proof, and we develop largely unconscious core beliefs out of these assumptions. Core beliefs have structural components such as boundary protection and are strongly glued together by the force we have labeled "synergy." In the case of my reaction to the Jehovah's Witnesses in Russia, I think it was the combination of their absolute unfamiliarity as a group (I have never known a Witness personally) combined with what seemed to be a double dose of "foreignness" (foreign country combined with foreign worship practices) that caused the immediate stiffening of my own existential boundaries. That I also immediately hung the label "victims" on the Russians further illustrates how quickly stereotyping can pick up a moral edge. And that a Russian Orthodox ceremony would have called up contrasting feelings of admiration seems to me additional evidence that something other than rational thought was taking place—after all, I had been confirmed in a liturgical church, so liturgical worship forms are obviously "good."

We have been noting throughout this discussion that we bring to each other not only our conscious awareness but also our belief systems. And these influence our reactions to political, social, personal, and religious systems, *in largely irrational ways*, as my example demonstrates. We are aware of this when it comes to racial and ethnic prejudices; there has been so much education directed at these challenges to our personal boundaries that most of us can recognize them when they occur. We are much less sensitive to our prejudices in the area of beliefs and religions, and this is particularly unfortunate when the collective mental health professions are (or should be) so directly involved with the belief systems of clients.

At the beginning of this discussion, I asked you to notice when a description or suggestion caused irritation. Do you know what peculiar combinations of beliefs and practices cause your own existential boundaries to stiffen? If you have undergone traditional analytic training, you are probably sensitized to the kinds of psychological issues that evoke negative countertransference. Are you equally aware of existential stances, as ifs, that "get your goat"? I personally have problems with clients who are absolute atheists. Can you work with atheists and encourage them to express their beliefs? Can you work with wholehearted Catholics? With Jewish radicals? With Christian fundamentalists?

I am advocating that mental health professionals must be as aware of their own core beliefs, whether these are secular or religious, as they are of other aspects of their personal lives. I have suggested that belief systems affect not only the psychological approach that seems congenial to us but also the ways in which we and our clients organize the chaos of our lives and reduce the angst that is an unavoidable condition of human awareness. When I interact with a client, I draw on my own inner life, *including my beliefs,* and elicit the client's. But if as a professional, I bracket off my beliefs, so probably will my client. For better or worse, my belief system causes me to hold the intellectual theories I do and to use the professional techniques I do, whether I am aware of it or not. Belief systems inevitably influence the ways in which we all interact, and differences between belief systems are unavoidable because our lives and experiences differ; we can never assume that the client shares the belief system of the professional. But intervention will be effective only if the professional first listens carefully and then understands sensitively what the belief system has meant to the individual.

Philosophical Conclusions

This book could not have been written thirty years ago. New scientific paradigms have cast suggestive light on traditional religious and psychological assumptions, and a new conception of ourselves as involved in some way in the creation of reality is causing us to rethink our understanding of the human person. So long as we humans were thought to be merely objects in a world of objects, our imaginations could be seen as adaptive mechanisms without transcendental significance; religion could be dismissed as an archaic construct, an old-fashioned notion that had been superseded by science; and therapists could be seen as fixers of broken personalities, mechanics of the human machine. But if it turns out that objects themselves are adaptive projections and that *consciousness* is primary, then religious experiences and therapeutic insights can again be viewed as more than merely adaptive forms of electrical thought impulses, and the various patterns of transcendental experience will once again be taken seriously.

We have assumed in this discussion that reality is not merely imposed on us from "out there" but rather that the way we organize our experience influences the very nature of reality itself. Just as every human being is a unique creation, we interact with the "out there" in a vast array of possible ways, and our diversity and our reactions provide richness and strengths that should be explored and respected—indeed, our diversity may be the key to a new *level* of reality.

Therapeutic Conclusions

We noted earlier that the two commonalities that psychology and religion share are the importance of relationship and the necessity for metaphors, and we observed that where religious resources are appealing to a client, they remain unparalleled sources of both. But in any case, enhancement of relationships and highlighting of the metaphors in dreams, artistic expression, and rituals should be part of any mental health intervention in which core beliefs have become an important component. I have suggested meditation and journaling as techniques for capturing life metaphors and intentional groups and retreat centers as new resources for sharing and relationship building.

We professionals are in the business of promoting mental health. But mental health is a slippery concept. When we refer to "clients," of whom are we speaking? The mentally ill? Fortunately, I think the term *mental illness* is much more appropriately and carefully used now than it was twenty years ago. Thanks perhaps to the insurance industry, which insists on careful diagnosis and documentation before it will dispense payments, the term has come to mean "ill" rather than "different." Every pastoral counselor, psychologist, and social worker must sometimes face up to the anguish of the genuinely mentally ill. As I have argued earlier, it is my strong conviction that mental illness is a medical problem. But those of us in the mental health business know that most of our time is spent with persons under stress, and that includes us all at one time or another. When we are under stress—divorce, loss of work, misfortune of various kinds—we may feel mentally ill. We may indeed feel physically ill as well; stress is hard on the machinery. But the condition is temporary, and the treatment requirements are entirely different than for people whose nervous or endocrine systems are causing their emotional turmoil.

Professionals should become life rafts, puzzle workers, problem identifiers, courage dispensers. I do not agree that we are in the business of solving problems—or not exclusively so—and I am particularly critical of the "quick fix" school of mental health treatment because I think above all that we are, or should be, what I could refer to as "centers of sanity," places where frazzled persons can ground themselves. People forget who they are when they are stressed. They forget what their coping skills used to be. They scare themselves to death. One of the greatest discoveries of my own educational pilgrimage was the variety of centers of sanity that is available; unfortunately, we in the mental health business have gotten stuck in the doctor's office, so to speak.

It seems important to say one last word about *discernment*. When I have presented these ideas to groups of mental health professionals, one question always arises: how do we identify belief systems that are truly destructive? My reply is in the form of another question: destructive to whom? As we have described, frequently the belief system being referred to is an evangelical or Pentecostal sect with rigid rules and guilt-producing dogmas. And though most professionals shudder at the finger-pointing quality of the life-style, we have suggested that for persons who have poor boundary protection, poor impulse control, and a culture of rage, such strongly constructed belief systems may provide exactly the emotional glue that is needed to keep them from falling into antisocial activity, criminal or otherwise violent behavior, or into the sort of depression we frequently see in marginal people (especially women) without hope. As was pointed out earlier, Pentecostal sects offer helpful structure for people whose internal rule-making capacity is impaired—emotional outlets within exciting worship services, plus clearly defined and externally imposed rules.

My personal criterion for discernment of evil derives from the theologian Gustavo Gutierrez: evil leads to death and powerlessness. If people are involved in a belief system that drains them of personal effectiveness (and my sense is that this is tricky; professionals need to beware of their own projections here) or is clearly damaging to their lives, then I think therapists are justified in trying to intervene.

Here again, knowledge of a variety of alternative belief systems should be an important part of a professional mental health person's arsenal. I made the suggestion earlier that mental health professionals educate themselves about the beliefs of various religious denominations, as well as the ways in which the religious community is organized, in order to be able to make knowledgeable referrals and to understand the religious inferences of their clients' stories. The overview presented in Chapter Thirteen is only a beginning and could be supplemented by on-site explorations in the community in which you live or work. Postgraduate educational opportunities to acquaint mental health professionals with religious resources could, and probably should, be made available by various professional organizations. A few years ago, mental health workers held workshops for clergy under the aegis of the community mental health movement. Perhaps the favor could be returned by the professionals in the religious community. In this discussion I have described a few of the many places where beliefs can be identified and affirmed. I am aware of having only scratched the surface, of having uncovered a veritable wealth of possibilities. I hope that we in the world of mental health will be able to help clients find their own spiritual resources, whether these are spiritual guides, family vacations at church camps, new courses of study, prayer partners, or small "house churches"—the possibilities are seemingly endless.

Living As If

It is not enough to live one's life morally, according to correct rules, nor is it enough to know "pop psychology" techniques for alleviating stress, however helpful these may sometimes be. It is not even enough to live life "happily," whatever that means. It is my conviction that we must, above all, live life as *fully* as we possibly can, as if we knew what truth and goodness and reality actually are. We should live courageously, creatively, and authentically, being true to our own natures and our own internal visions and, if possible, in community with companions who share our visions. Living fully does not mean living self-indulgently, no matter what core beliefs one espouses; I do not mean to present here narcissism with a religious face. It does mean living with our psychic antennae fully extended. It means not only experiencing painful places where old wounds remain unhealed and old questions unanswered but also facing into the future, finding places and people who can encourage our creative spirits and challenge our untapped talents. It means taking our dreams and flights of fancy seriously, responding to our inner voices, and reaching out to the unknown, the ephemeral.

The rationale for uncovering clients' diverse belief systems is found in the image of the elephant called reality, an unknown complexity of which any one of us has only a small knowledge and can describe only partially. Because reality seems complex beyond our wildest speculation, we can encompass multiple creative concepts about the structure of human life and personality and multiple creative concepts about the meaning of human existence without abandoning our own intellectual integrity. As we explore diverse experiments in personal and spiritual enrichment, we note that the enhancing of the personal can enhance the spiritual, and vice versa.

A new paradigm is beginning to emerge, a sort of existential tapestry. A pattern of universal meaning does not appear on the side that I can see—all I see are loose ends "of many bright colors to make our hearts cry" (to quote "De Colores," the theme song of the Cursillo movement). Perhaps a beautiful picture will appear when we are "on the other side"; perhaps not. But it seems to me that one reason why the great commandments in most religious traditions have to do with love, rather than with understanding and knowledge, is that when we love, we appreciate the unique other unconditionally, and we make room for that other to grow, whether the other is a person or a culture or a belief system. And we somehow incorporate the other into ourselves, thereby enriching both heaven and earth.

References

Allport, G. *Psychology and Religion*. New York: Basic Books, 1946.

Appleyard, B. *Understanding the Present*. New York: Doubleday, 1992.

Assagioli, R. *Psychosynthesis*. New York: Hobbs/Dorman, 1965.

Bakken, K. L. *The Call to Wholeness*. New York: Crossroad, 1985.

Bandler, R., and Grinder, J. *Frogs into Princes*. Moab, Utah: RealPeople Press, 1979.

Barbour, I. G. *Myths, Models, and Paradigms*. San Francisco: Harper, 1974.

Barry, W., and Connolly, W. *The Practice of Spiritual Direction*. New York: Seabury Press, 1982.

Bateson, G. *Steps to an Ecology of Mind*. New York: Ballantine Books, 1972.

Becker, E. *The Denial of Death*. New York: Free Press, 1973.

Becker, E. *Escape from Evil*. New York: Free Press, 1975.

Bellah, R., and others. *Habits of the Heart*. London: Hutchinson, 1988.

Berne, E. *Games People Play*. New York: Grove Press, 1964.

Bettleheim, B. *The Uses of Enchantment*. New York: Knopf, 1975.

Biddle, W. E. *Integration of Religion and Psychiatry*. New York: Macmillan, 1955.

Blanck, G., and Blanck, R. *Ego Psychology*. New York: Columbia University Press, 1974.

Boisen, A. *Religion in Crisis and Custom*. New York: HarperCollins, 1955. (Originally published 1945.)

Bolen, J. *The Tao of Psychology*. San Francisco: Harper, 1979.

Broughton, R. S. *Parapsychology: The Controversial Science*. New York: Ballantine Books, 1991.

Bry, A. *Inside Psychotherapy*. New York: Basic Books, 1972.

Buber, M. *I and Thou*. New York: Charles Scribner's Sons, 1970.

Capelle, R. *Changing Human Systems*. Toronto: International Human Systems Institute, 1979.

Capra, F. *The Turning Point*. New York: Bantam Books, 1983.

Capra, F., and Stendl-Rast, D. *Belonging to the Universe*. San Francisco: Harper, 1992.

Cone, J. *My Soul Looks Back*. Nashville, Tenn.: Abington Press, 1982.

Davies, P. *God and the New Physics*. New York: Simon & Schuster, 1983.

Diehl, W. E. *In Search of Faithfulness*. Minneapolis: Augsburg Fortress, 1987.

Donner, J. "Faith in Perspective." Unpublished paper, University of Michigan, 1980.

Douglas, M., and Tipton, S. (eds.). *Religion and America*. Boston: Beacon Press, 1982.

Dumoulin, H., and Maraldo, J. C. (eds.). *Buddhism in the Modern World*. New York: Macmillan, 1976.

Durnbaugh, D. F. *The Believers' Church*. New York: Macmillan, 1968.

Dych, W. "Theology in a New Key." In J. L. O'Donovan (ed.), *A World of Grace*. New York: Crossroad, 1984.

Dyson, F. *Infinite in All Directions*. New York: HarperCollins, 1988.

Edwards, T. *Spiritual Friend*. Mahwah, N.J.: Paulist Press, 1980.

Edwards, T. *Living in the Presence*. San Francisco: Harper, 1987.

Ferucci, P. *What We May Be*. Los Angeles: Tarcher, 1976.

Finke, R., and Stark, R. *The Churching of America, 1776–1990*. New Brunswick, N.J.: Rutgers University Press, 1992.

Fox, M. *Original Blessing*. Santa Fe, N.M.: Bear, 1984.

Frankl, V. E. *Man's Search for Meaning*. Boston: Beacon Press, 1992. (Originally published 1959.)

Freud, S. *An Outline of Psychoanalysis*. New York: Norton, 1949.

Friedman, L. *Meetings with Remarkable Women*. Boston: Shambhala, 1987.

Fuller, B. *Critical Path*. New York: St. Martin's Press, 1981.

Ganter, G., and Yeakel, M. *Human Behavior and the Social Environment*. New York: Columbia University Press, 1980.

Geertz, C. *Interpretation of Cultures*. New York: Basic Books, 1973.

Gutierrez, G. *We Drink from Our Own Wells*. Los Angeles: Orbis Publications, 1985.

Haley, J. *Uncommon Therapy*. New York: Norton, 1973.

Haughton, R. *The Transformation of Man*. Springfield, Ill.: Templegate, 1967.

Holmes, U., III. *A History of Christian Spirituality*. New York: Seabury Press, 1980.

Holmes, U., III. *Ministry and Imagination*. New York: Seabury Press, 1984.

Holtz, B. W. *Guide to Jewish Books*. New York: Schocken Books, 1992.

Howe, R. *The Miracle of Dialogue*. New York: Seabury Press, 1963.

Howes, E. *Intersection and Beyond*. San Francisco: Guild for Psychological Studies, 1971.

Hugel, F. *Eternal Life*. Edinburgh, Scotland: Clark, 1912.

James, W. *The Varieties of Religious Experience*. New York: New American Library, 1958. (Originally published 1902.)

Joy, W. B. *Joy's Way*. Los Angeles: Tarcher, 1979.

Jung, C. G. *Modern Man in Search of a Soul*. New York: Harvest, 1955. (Originally published 1933.)

Kaplan, L. (ed.). *Fundamentalism in Comparative Perspective*. Amherst: University of Massachusetts Press, 1992.

Keen, S. *The Passionate Life*. San Francisco: Harper, 1983.

Keen, S. *The Faces of the Enemy*. San Francisco: Harper, 1986.

Keen, S. *To a Dancing God*. San Francisco: Harper, 1990.

Kelsey, M. *Adventure Inward*. Minneapolis: Augsburg Fortress, 1979a.

Kelsey, M. *Discernment*. Mahwah, N.J.: Paulist Press, 1979b.

Kelsey, M. *Companions on the Inner Way*. New York: Crossroad, 1984.

Kennedy, E. *On Becoming a Counselor*. New York: Continuum, 1977.

Kerr, H. T., and Mulder, J. M. *Conversions*. Grand Rapids, Mich.: Eerdmans, 1983.

Kertzer, M. N. *What Is a Jew?* New York: Collier Books, 1978.

Kierkegaard, S. *The Sickness Unto Death*. New York: Doubleday, 1954. (Originally published 1849.)

Kung, H. *Does God Exist?* New York: Vintage Books, 1981.

Leech, K. *Soul Friend*. London: Sheldon Press, 1977.

Leech, K. *Experiencing God*. San Francisco: Harper, 1985.

LeShan, L. *The Medium, the Mystic, and the Physicist*. New York: Ballantine Books, 1966.

LeShan, L. *Alternate Realities*. New York: Evans, 1976.

Levine, S. *Healing into Life and Death*. Garden City, N.Y.: Anchor Press/Doubleday, 1987.

Lewis, C. S. *The Problem of Pain*. New York: Macmillan, 1959.

Lewis, C. S. *The Four Loves*. New York: Macmillan, 1960.

Lewis, C. S. *Mere Christianity*. New York: Macmillan, 1978. (Originally published 1952.)

Linn, D., and Linn, M. *Healing of Memories*. Mahwah, N.J.: Paulist Press, 1974.

Lowen, A. *The Language of the Body*. New York: Macmillan, 1958.

Mann, R. *The Light of Consciousness*. Albany: State University of New York Press, 1984.

Marty, M. *Pilgrims in Their Own Land*. Boston: Little, Brown, 1984.

Marty, M. *Religion and Republic*. Boston: Beacon Press, 1987a.

Marty, M. *A Short History of Christianity*. Minneapolis: Augsburg Fortress, 1987b.

Marty, M., and Appleby, S. *The Glory and the Power*. Boston: Beacon Press, 1992.

Maslow, A. *Toward a Psychology of Being*. New York: Van Nostrand, 1962.

Maslow, A. "The Farther Reaches of Human Nature." *Journal of Transpersonal Psychology*, 1969, *1*, 1–9.

Maslow, A. *Religion, Values, and Peak Experiences*. New York: Viking Penguin, 1976. (Originally published 1970.)

May, G. *Pilgrimage Home*. Mahwah, N.J.: Paulist Press, 1979.

May, G. *Will and Spirit*. New York: HarperCollins, 1982.

May, R. *The Courage to Create*. New York: Norton, 1975.

May, R. *The Discovery of Being*. New York: Norton, 1983.

May, R. *The Cry for Myth*. New York: Norton, 1991.

Meissner, W. W. *Psychoanalysis and Religious Experience*. New Haven, Conn.: Yale University Press, 1984.

Melton, J. G. *The Encyclopedia of American Religions*. Detroit: Gale Research, 1988.

Menninger, K. *Love Against Hate*. Orlando, Fla.: Harcourt Brace, 1970.
Merton, T. *Mystics and Zen Masters*. New York: Noonday, 1967. (Originally published 1961.)
Mitchell, H. H., and Lewter, N. C. *Soul Theology*. San Francisco: Harper, 1986.
Moore, T. *Care of the Soul*. New York: HarperCollins, 1992.
Moreal, D. *Buddhist America*. Santa Fe, N.M.: John Muir Publications, 1988.
Moyers, B. *Healing and the Mind*. New York: Doubleday, 1993.
Murphy, C. "Who Do Men Say I Am?" *Atlantic Monthly*, Dec. 1986, pp. 37–59.
Needleman, J. *The New Religions*. Garden City, N.Y.: Doubleday, 1970.
Needleman, J., and Baker, G. *Understanding the New Religions*. New York: Seabury Press, 1978.
Neufelder, J. M., and Coelho, M. C. *Writings in Spiritual Direction*. New York: Seabury Press, 1982.
O'Connor, E. *Our Many Selves*. New York: HarperCollins, 1971.
O'Donovan, L. J. (ed.). *A World of Grace*. New York: Crossroad, 1984.
Olsen, C. M. *Cultivating Religious Growth Groups*. Philadelphia: The Westminster Press, 1984.
Orstein, R. (ed.). *The Nature of Human Consciousness*. New York: W. H. Freeman, 1975.
Pearce, J. C. *The Crack in the Cosmic Egg*. New York: Pocket Books, 1971.
Peck, M. S. *The Road Less Traveled*. New York: Simon & Schuster, 1978.
Peck, M. S. *The People of the Lie*. New York: Simon & Schuster, 1983.
Peck, M. S. *World Waiting to Be Born*. New York: Bantam Books, 1993.
Polster, E. *Every Person's Life Is Worth a Novel*. New York: Norton, 1987.
Polster, E., and Polster, M. *Gestalt Therapy Integrated*. New York: Brunner/Mazel, 1973.
Postema, D. *Space for God*. Minneapolis: Augsburg Fortress, 1983.
Progoff, I. *The Practice of Process Meditation*. New York: Dialogue House Library, 1980.
Rahner, K. *Foundations of Christian Faith*. New York: Crossroad, 1984.
Raphael, M. L. *Profiles in American Judaism*. San Francisco: Harper, 1985.
Rifkin, A. "Looking Inward." *Friends Journal*, 1986, *32* (13), 10–12.
Rogers, C. *On Becoming a Person*. Boston: Houghton Mifflin, 1961.
Rosten, L. (ed.). *Religions of America*. New York: Simon & Schuster, 1975.
Sanford, J. *The Kingdom Within*. Philadelphia: Lippincott, 1966.
Santa-Maria, M. L. *Growth Through Meditation and Journal Writing*. Mahwah, N.J.: Paulist Press, 1983.
Searle, J. R. *The Rediscovery of the Mind*. Cambridge, Mass.: MIT Press, 1992.
Sheinkin, D. *Path of the Kabbalah*. New York: Paragon House, 1986.
Sipe, A.W.R., and Rowe, C. J. (eds.). *Psychiatry, Ministry, and Pastoral Counseling*. Collegeville, Minn.: Liturgical Press, 1984.
Skinner, B. F. *Science and Human Behavior*. New York: Macmillan, 1953.
Stokes, K. (ed.). *Faith Development in the Adult Life Cycle*. New York: Sadlier, 1982.

Suzuki, S. *Zen Mind, Beginner's Mind*. New York: Weatherhill, 1994. (Originally published 1970.)

Szaz, T. *The Myth of Mental Illness*. New York: Ell, 1961.

Tart, C. (ed.). *Transpersonal Psychologies*. New York: HarperCollins, 1975.

Teilhard de Chardin, P. *The Divine Milieu*. New York: Harper/Colophon, 1960.

Teilhard de Chardin, P. *The Heart of Matter*. Orlando, Fla.: Harcourt Brace, 1978.

Tenzin, G. (Dalai Lama). *The Meaning of Life*. Boston: Wisdom, 1992.

Tillich, P. *Systematic Theology, Vol. I*. Chicago: University of Chicago Press, 1951.

Tournier, P. *Creative Suffering*. San Francisco: Harper, 1981.

Van Franz, M. L. *On Divination and Synchronicity*. Toronto: Inner City Books, 1980.

Vanier, J. *Community and Growth*. Mahwah, N.J.: Paulist Press, 1979.

Watts, A. *Psychotherapy East and West*. New York: Vintage Books, 1975. (Originally published 1961.)

Wicks, R. J., Parsons, R. D., and Capps, D. E. (eds.). *Clinical Handbook of Pastoral Counseling*. Mahwah, N.J.: Paulist Press, 1985.

Wilbur, K. *No Boundary*. Boston: New Science Library, 1979.

Wink, W. *Naming the Powers*. Minneapolis: Augsburg Fortress, 1986.

Wuthrow, R. *The Restructuring of American Religion*. Princeton, N.J.: Princeton University Press, 1988.

Yalom, I. *Existential Psychotherapy*. New York: Basic Books, 1980.

Zinker, J. *Creative Process in Gestalt Therapy*. New York: Brunner/Mazel, 1977.

Index

━

A

Alcoholics Anonymous, 62, 165
American Friends Service Committee, 139
Amish, 120
Analytical psychology, 62–63, 66–67
Anglican churches, 135
Angst, 13; reducing, 13–15
Anxiety, 14–15
Appleyard, B., 46, 112
As ifs, 49, 50; implications of, 77–90; psychological, 61–68; religious, 71–76, 100–107; secular, 53–60, 91–100. *See also* Belief systems
Assagioli, R., 162
Assessment, 83–84
Assumptions, 8. *See also* Beliefs
Atheism, 54–56; counseling with, 92–93; influence of, on therapy, 18–19
Authority, as dimension of worship, 130–131
Awareness. *See* Moral awareness; Self-awareness

B

Becker, E., 14, 116–117, 155
Behavior therapy, 63–64
Behaviorism, 61–62, 63–64
Belief systems, 7, 11–12, 20; aspects of reality addressed by, 21–22; boundary protection with, 28–31; counseling with religious, 100–107; counseling with secular, 91–100; definition of, 7; discerning destructive, 171–172; diversity of, 22–26; good and evil within, 48; need to understand, 8–9; purposes of, 12–16; of religion and psychology, 16, 50–51; and stages of counseling, 80–87; synergy of, 26–28; therapy influenced by, 18–19.

See also As ifs; Religious belief systems
Beliefs: alternative, about ethics, 47–49; alternative, about reality, 45–47; about nature of human being, 49–51; versus religion, 8. *See also* Core beliefs
Biersdorf, J., 97, 130, 158
Body therapies, 67–68
Boisen, A., 6
Boundary protection: of belief systems, 28–31; of core beliefs, 125; counseling with belief in, 105–107
Branch Davidians, 119
Broughton, R. S., 45, 46, 47
Buddhists, 135, 138. *See also* Eastern religions

C

Capra, F., 47
Catholic Workers, 104
Chaos, mediating, 15–16
Charitable activities, of religions, 139
Christian Scientists, 118
Christianity: cocreationism of, 73–74; as dualistic, 41; educational institutions of, 138; evangelical, 75–76; fundamentalism in, 114. *See also* Religion, American
Church of the Savior (Washington, D.C.), 105
Churches: atheists in, 55–56; changing nature of American, 135–136; with cocreationist beliefs, 104–105; mental health professionals' ignorance of, 133–134; unaffiliated, 139. *See also* Religious systems
Clergy. *See* Authority
Cocreationism, 73–75; counseling with belief in, 103–105
Conversion: counseling clients with, 101, 102; experience of, 73; omission of

mention of, 153; as tool for therapy, 73. *See also* Revelational experience

Core beliefs: example of influence of, 43–44; professionals' awareness of, 168–169; reason for discussing, 9; religous context for, 133–139. *See also* Beliefs

Counseling: avoiding spirituality in, 151–152; belief systems and stages of, 80–87; in nontraditional settings, 87–89; with religious beliefs, 100–107; with secular beliefs, 91–100. *See also* Therapy

Counselors. *See* Mental health professionals

Craziness, 141, 145

Cults, 118–120

D

Death: core beliefs about, 77–79; counseling before, 151–152; fear of, 14, 116–117; nontraditional intervention experience with, 87–88

Denial: as consistent with belief system, 19; religion as, 116

Dialoguing, as therapy technique, 163–164

Discernment, 119; of cults, 118–120; of destructive belief systems, 171–172

Diversity: of belief systems, 22–26; and ritual, 129

Donner, J., 12

Douglas, M., 114

Dreams, therapeutic interest in, 36–37

Duality, 37, 38; versus unity, 37–40

Dyson, F., 24, 47

E

Eastern religions, 40, 41, 114. *See also* Buddhists

Edwards, H., 61, 161, 162

Edwards, T., 6, 163

Ethics, alternative view of, 47–49

Evangelical Christianity, 75–76. *See also* Fundamentalism

F

Finke, R., 115

Fowler, J., 136

Fox, M., 74

Frankl, V. E., 153

Free association, 161

Freud, S., 61–62, 64–65, 116

Fuller, B., 26

Fundamentalism: boundary protection in, 106–107; resurgence of, 114. *See also* Evangelical Christianity

G

Geddes, F., 97

Geertz, C., 111

God: American belief in, 133; as ifs involving belief in, 71–76; concepts of, 16–19; dialoguing technique with, 164; importance of follow-up on, 83

Goldstein, K., 14

Good and evil. *See* Ethics

Group therapies, 65, 165

Guided imagery, 162

Gutierrez, G., 171

H

Happiness, atheists' search for, 55, 56, 92–93

Hinduism. *See* Eastern religions

Holmes, Urban, III, 73, 131

Howes, E., 123

Humanism, 56–58, 60; counseling with, 93–97; versus atheism, 93

Humanistic psychology, 62, 64, 65

I

Ignatius of Loyola, 156, 161; journaling technique of, 159

Intervention, reinforcing belief systems in, 84–86

Islam: as dualistic, 41, 137; fundamentalism in, 114. *See also* Muslims

J

James, W., 45, 62, 68, 72

Jefferson, T., 55

Jehovah's Witnesses, prejudicial reaction to, 167

Journaling, 156–157; Ignatius of Loyola on, 159; Kelsey on, 159–160, 164; Progoff on, 157–158